Abbé René Laurentin is Professor of Theology at the University of Angers and a *peritus* at the Vatican Council. During World War II he was decorated with the Croix de Guerre, was taken prisoner, and taught Hebrew in a POW camp. After the war he earned the Docteur ès lettres with high honors from the Sorbonne, and the Docteur en théologie from the Institut Catholique of Paris. He is the author of three volumes on the Vatican Council, as well as books on Marian theology, Lourdes, and the Gospel of St. Luke.

The Question of Mary

The Question
of Mary

by RENÉ LAURENTIN

Translated from the French by I. G. PIDOUX
Preface by HILDA GRAEF

HOLT, RINEHART AND WINSTON

NEW YORK   CHICAGO   SAN FRANCISCO

Published in England under the title
Mary's Place in the Church

English translation copyright © 1965 by Burns & Oates Ltd.

Published in French under the title *La Question Mariale*
Copyright © 1963 by Editions du Seuil

Library of Congress Catalog Card Number: 65-12075

NIHIL OBSTAT : ANDREAS J. MOORE, L.C.L.

CENSOR DEPUTATUS

IMPRIMATUR : PATRITIUS CASEY

VICARIUS GENERALIS

WESTMONASTERII : DIE 2a NOVEMBRIS 1964

The Nihil obstat *and* Imprimatur *are a declaration that a book or pamphlet
is considered to be free from doctrinal or moral error. It is not implied that those
who have granted the* Nihil obstat *and* Imprimatur *agree with the contents,
opinions or statements expressed.*

First Edition

85168-0115

Printed in Great Britain

Foreword

EVER since the Reformation the Catholic attitude to the Mother of Jesus has been a very controversial issue, calling forth both abuse and exaggerations. On the one hand, every honour paid to her by Catholics was regarded as idolatry by their opponents, on the other Catholics often went too far in their fervour by claiming "privileges" for her that actually belonged only to her Son. Only during the last few years, in the course of the Ecumenical Movement, have serious efforts been made on both sides to come to a better understanding of the true place of Mary in the Christian faith.

Therefore the present book by the well-known French mariologist is particularly welcome, for it presents an authoritative discussion of the whole Marian question in Catholic doctrine and devotion. For there has not only been the violent opposition between Protestants and Catholics (including the Orthodox) on this subject, there has also been a divergence of attitudes within the Catholic Church itself. Owing to what Laurentin calls "the dissociation of theology and life" in the later Middle Ages, there has been a centuries-old division between the so-called maximalist and minimalist schools of mariological thought.

Because with the decline of scholasticism theology became increasingly abstract and divorced from life, the faithful turned by way of compensation to a Marian devotion devoid of a sane theological basis. Thus there developed an attitude to the Mother of God inspired by the adage: *De Maria numquam satis* (there can never be enough of Mary) and intent only on heaping more and more honours on her, regardless of whether these were in keeping with her state as a creature, however exalted. The theologians, on the other hand, lost interest in mariological questions and thus left Marian devotion to grow as it would, without checking undesirable developments.

Laurentin's book shows a way out of this dilemma by proposing a principle which will enable both theology and devotion to steer clear of the pitfalls of "minimalizing" and "maximalizing". It is this, that in, through and for Christ Mary is totally relative to God and totally correlative to the Church. It follows from this maxim that there are certain limits which must be respected in a sane view of the person and office of the Blessed Virgin. Unlike her Son, she is fully (that is to say only) human; she was redeemed, she neither pre-existed before her conception nor enjoyed the beatific vision, and, being a woman, she had no hierarchical functions. Further, Laurentin gives a very perspicacious and highly necessary analysis of certain papal documents which are often used in mariological books as infallible pronouncements which may not be gainsaid, whereas they are but private opinions, often coloured by devotional purposes, of the pope in question and do not involve papal infallibility at all.

In his very valuable chapter on The Ecumenical Problem, moreover, Laurentin shows up our differences in the eirenical spirit that pervades the whole book; it ought to be welcomed by Protestants and Orthodox alike.

Since the Marian question has been discussed by the Council this book is very timely, but it is more than that. It will remain valid for many years to come. For it presents an eminently sane and balanced view of a very difficult subject and gives the Mother of God her rightful place which must reflect, in the words of Laurentin, "both the glory and the humility". It is the glory which our Protestant brethren have so often neglected; it is the humility which we Catholics have only too frequently disregarded. In stressing and explaining both in his excellent book, Abbé Laurentin has done a great service both to Catholicism and Oecumenism.

HILDA GRAEF

Oxford

Contents

Contents

8

I

The Present Situation:
Crest or Crisis?

THE position which the Virgin Mary has assumed in the Catholic Church of the present day is one of extraordinary prominence. This movement culminated in the Marian Years celebrated towards the end of Pius XII's pontificate with the definition of the dogma of the Assumption in 1950, the centenary of the definition of the Immaculate Conception in 1954, and the centenary of Lourdes in 1958.

1. THE EXTENT OF THE CONTEMPORARY MARIAN MOVEMENT

The study and comparison of a few facts and figures will show us both the extent and also the recent development of the movement.

The principal pilgrimages of the Middle Ages had as their object Christ or the apostles—the Holy Land, the Holy Sepulchre, St James of Compostela, Rome where the "confessions" of St Peter and St Paul then held a place now, unfortunately, sadly neglected. Today the pilgrimages which draw the largest crowds are those to the shrines of our Lady: two and a half million pilgrims every year go to Lourdes alone, and very large numbers to Fatima, too. To these two shrines could be added hundreds of others: Saragossa and Montserrat in Spain, Chartres and Le Puy, La Salette and Pontmain in France, Loreto and Monteberico, Syracuse and Tre Fontane[1] in Italy, Banneux and Beauraing in Belgium, Einsiedeln in Switzerland, Mariazell in Austria, Maria Laach in Germany, Czestochowa in Poland, Aparecida in Brazil, Lujan in the Argentine, our Lady of Guadalupe in Mexico, to quote only a few of those which are so well known as to draw a large number of pilgrims from many nations.

Many of these names, in fact all of those where the pilgrimage is of recent origin, bring another interesting fact before us. In earlier times the appearances were principally of Christ, but for the last hundred and fifty years it is almost exclusively apparitions of the Blessed Virgin without Christ[2] which have taken such a large place in Christian piety.

The foundation of Marian groups and institutions has greatly increased. Nearly all the women's orders which have appeared in the Church over the last century and a half have been dedicated to our Lady. There are so many of them that Fr Bergh, who wrote a monograph on the question, had to give up the attempt to count them. The incomplete figures which he collected speak for themselves: 11 foundations in 1835, 16 in 1850, 14 in 1854 ("record years"). Although the figures for this century are not so high, there were still 24 between 1920 and 1929.[3]

Alongside the classic types of Marian associations (confraternities, archconfraternities and congregations which still exist in large numbers) the twentieth century has seen the appearance of mass groupings which set out to perform some militant action of a specifically Marian character. There is the Militia of the Immaculate Conception founded in 1917 by Fr Kolbe, which can count more than two million adherents. The Legion of Mary founded by Frank Duff in 1921 has millions of members in a thousand dioceses. The Blue Army founded in 1947 calculated its effective strength at 15 million in 1959.[4] Every year sees a host of new efforts: "crusades" with various objectives, consecrations, coronations or translations of statues, like the "Great Return",[5] etc. The *Marianum* Centre in Rome undertook to keep a record of them all in a series of yearbooks which appear under the title *Ragguaglio Mariano*. The edition for the 1954 Marian Year had 625 pages and does not claim to be exhaustive!

Among the most significant developments are the Marian Congresses which made a sporadic appearance at the end of the nineteenth century, and which in the twentieth have developed on three levels—the regional, the national and the international. The following figures for the last few years include only those which have produced published work:[6]

3 in 1947	11 in 1951
4 in 1948	10 in 1952
7 in 1949	11 in 1953
15 in 1950	43 in 1954

6 in 1955   4 in 1957
5 in 1956   More than 10 in 1958

But the most remarkable of all the features of the present-day Marian movement is the effort in the field of doctrine which animates it. Since 1934, nine national societies of Marian studies and an international academy have been created. In several universities, chairs or even associated Marian academies or institutes have been founded. Numerous theses are defended there. Specialist Marian libraries have multiplied on both sides of the Atlantic of which several contain about 10,000 volumes. The Banneux library, recently moved to Louvain, is on the point of passing 20,000. Two Marian reviews of a strictly theological character have been founded in the last thirty years and around these are grouped many devotional and pastoral periodicals.

Never has so much been written about our Lady. Father Besutti in his specialized bibliographies cites the following figures : [7]

982 titles in 1948-9
2,209 titles in 1950-1
5,758 titles in 1952-7.

In round figures this is a thousand a year, and it does not include more popular non-scientific periodicals. In spite of this omission the author confesses frankly that he is overwhelmed by this material, which, as he writes, "knows no limits".

This high yield is normally the source of unqualified satisfaction in specialist circles. It is seen as full of promise—the dawn of a Marian era. Did not heaven itself give the signal with the apparitions of the nineteenth century? The weighty support of the Supreme Magisterium of the Church, so productive of encyclicals on this subject, must surely guarantee the authenticity of the "Marian movement". How can the two definitions of Pius IX and Pius XII be anything but an infallible endorsement of the movement and at the same time an augur of yet further activities?

2. Grounds for Disquiet

If we look only at these external signs of prosperity (which anyway have seen some setbacks in more recent years), we shall overlook the existence of some real problems which did not escape Pius XII himself. The Marian fervour and piety of this pope accompanied a concern for a true sense of proportion, a reticence which astonished some mariologists, and a moderating influence in which he carried on the ancient tradition of the Holy See in the matter. Pius XII was very guarded about the dogmatization of Mary as the mediatrix and co-redemptrix, for he did not wish to do anything which might veil the transcendence of the *unus Mediator*. He systematically avoided the title co-redemptrix in his pontifical acts, and in his directives to the Marian theologians was careful to warn against exaggeration as well as against understatement.

John XXIII adopted the moderating directives of his predecessor and issued some new ones for the diocese of Rome. In an allocution to his clergy he put them on their guard against a tendency

> to cultivate certain excessive practices and special devotions in the cult of the Madonna . . . devotions which at times give a poor idea of the piety of our good people. . . . Certain pious practices satisfy only the emotions, but they do not suffice for the fulfilling of religious obligations, and correspond even less to the first three weighty and imperious commandments of the Decalogue.

On another occasion, at the close of the Synod, he said in his address :

> The experience of the first year . . . of the new Bishop of Rome . . . has given him the feeling that certain souls make use of special devotions, new titles and a cult of local inspiration and character, which give the impression of leaving the field free to phantasy with little room for the concentrated activity of the soul. We would invite you to keep to what is simplest and most ancient in the practice of the Church.[8]

The truth is that anyone who follows the present Marian movement closely finds ground not only for admiration, but also for reservations and perplexity.

The abundance of publications and opinions

The sheer abundance of voices is one of the Marian movement's chief characteristics. The proliferation of viewpoints would be supportable if they were all of value, but the multitude of publications includes many of no value or at least of very little. Louis Veuillot passed the following severe judgment on the Marian literature of the nineteenth century (when the numerical tide was already in full flood):

> In the immense quantity of volumes that are produced each year, it is hard to find even a handful that are not completely unsatisfactory: awkward, cold declamations, badly written texts, lessons with no doctrine, with no love, and too often with no grammar. It is astonishing that the zeal which moves people to read such stuff seems to provide such little inspiration to those who write it.[9]

The situation has certainly improved. Declamatory statements are all but out of fashion nowadays, and thought has become more organized. Nevertheless, there are still echoes of that situation. Approximations, superfluities, platitudes, writings with no substance—none of these has disappeared completely.[10] Recently, at the home of a fellow mariologist, I was looking at the shelves of books awaiting review. It was a depressing experience. In the scientific as well as in the literary world the law both of honour and of practical necessity is contained in the aphorism: write nothing which is not necessary, irreplaceable in fact. Everything else is superfluous and is not fit to see the light of day. On those heavily laden shelves there was so little that was really necessary!

In the field of spiritual literature, the irreplaceable is that which brings a renewed concept of the mystery, a new note, fresh ways of stating ideas, and not simply the attempt to sustain artificially an unnatural piety.

In the field of theology, the irreplaceable is either the scientific editing of sources still unpublished or incorrectly edited, or a work of research with the following characteristics. First, method; and implicit in that is a double requirement: to take over all former work on the matter in question, to exploit fully all available resources (texts, methods of investigation) and thus to advance the subject as far as possible. But this is not all, for far beyond mere method, science presupposes, as its very mainspring, an approach capable of bringing to light, out of the ill-defined and confused mass of possible knowledge, a subject until

13

then neglected, poorly understood or ill defined, a subject to which little attention had been paid and whose elucidation will open the way to further progress. Think for example of the research to find a unifying theory which brought about Einstein's discovery, a subject on which he continued to work, without success but not without reason, during the remaining years of his life.

I am not claiming that theology must be assimilated to natural science. In it discoveries are less startling for they deal with a deposit already definitively constituted and transmitted by *tradition*. But it is nevertheless true that the full understanding and elucidation of what this deposit contains provides a vast field for investigation, and that, here as everywhere else, method and approach are primary conditions of success and of the quality of the work.

Exegesis, to take one example, took on a more scientific attitude when it discovered the human dimension of the divinely inspired books, their literary forms, and, together with these, the systems of investigation which use the comparative method between the various parts of the Bible themselves and also extra-biblical material. These discoveries have opened up avenues of progress whose limits are still indiscernible.

In Marian theology the first requirement of this method, the assimilation of all the work already done, is discouraged by the abundance of the specialized literature. For my part, I narrowly missed being bogged down at my first attempt. I had chosen a minimal subject on which, I had been told, there was "nothing in tradition". After much condensing, I emerged with an historical work 680 pages long.[11] The sheer overabundance of these last years has made the task even more onerous: specialized bibliographies exhaust themselves in the effort to present a simple index of publications; Marian reviews which had cheerfully made it their intention to give the abridged contents of the articles scattered throughout the theological reviews of the whole world, have had to give up under the sheer weight of material. The task is made all the more delicate because the assessment of relative values is hindered by sociological factors: good relations and courtesies tend to reduce the worth one can attribute to most of the reviews which ought themselves to reduce the work. The picture is further confused because, at the rate of work today, several studies on the same subject will appear, sometimes simultaneously, without any reference to one another. Thus the year 1954 alone saw the appearance of half-a-dozen monographs on the problem of the Immaculate Conception in St Augustine, and the points of view in each are so different that it would seem quicker to begin all over again in a new effort rather than to take account of the paths followed by these six solitary knights, each of them carving his own way across the country.

If we continue down this slope of unco-ordinated abundance, what happened in the eighteenth century will happen again : a general lassitude, a falling-off of interest. A gigantic effort, of which better things could have been expected, will end with neither glory nor profit.

However that may be, the second requirement of methodic study (that is, to find a new approach or technique to solve the problem presented) is compromised by the effort involved in getting beyond the first. So instead of developing along new lines which might lead out of the present dead-ends, a great number of studies are content with an erudition which does nothing more than stir up the dust of some older works.

But the greatest lack, in the whole mass of Marian publications, is without doubt that direction of outlook which alone can provoke a new approach to the problems and open up the way to any real progress. Too often the most conventional problems are minutely re-examined. In many Marian monographs the particular interest of the author who is being studied (if such an interest exists) seems to be ignored, and all they do is to draw up a list of any contributions the person in question made or could make to the composition of the theses catalogued in modern manuals of mariology. Often this has the effect of increasing the very obstacles which need to be cleared away.

On the other hand, few mariologists have been inspired to seek for the secret of the balance and clarity which are found in the Marian doctrine and piety of the East. More have been fired by the ecclesiological aspect of the problem, but the results make it seem that a part of the effort spent on this has been used in neutralizing any fruitful or stimulating effects this line of thought might seem to offer. This is no isolated case. More than one study with a fine outward appearance spends itself in a furious effort which results in mixing up and obscuring once again subjects which previous studies had courageously sorted out. I am thinking of such cases as that of the patristic digest by Mgr Jouassard which a recent work has contradicted by finding the Assumption in the works of authors of the earliest centuries, and all the mariology of recent papal encyclicals in the African Fathers. Various mediaeval researches by Fr Barré have been similarly followed by studies which are partly regressive.

At a deeper level, mariology is often not sufficiently penetrated by that profound requirement of which the First Vatican Council spoke: the double relationship of theology to the whole of the mystery and to the salvation of men, a subject to which we shall return.

In these conditions, the mariologists' ambition to be "scientific" is borne out in a small number of publications only. Elsewhere the exterior apparatus of science (notes, references, bibliographies) is doubtless found, but not that method and orientation which are essential to it.

Despite several efforts, the co-ordination of this mass of studies remains unsatisfactory. In our day the death-knell of individual scientific studies has sounded, yet theology has scarcely entered on the path of collective work, the method of our times in those fields where there is progress: nuclear physics, or sociology, for example. Except for a few groups given to producing critical editions, and the praiseworthy attempts of the Marian Academy or the Marian Institute of the Servites in Rome, individual studies are still the rule of the day. Congresses and other brief meetings, and the growing number of publications in the form of "symposia", are only a palliative. Isolated efforts are put side by side, but they are not organized to be of service to some enterprise in scale with the age.

In short, even if Marian work in the last few years has produced some important results, it has been impossible for anyone to follow as a whole. It is beyond the ability of anyone to digest it all. The abundance of the Marian movement is, to a large extent, inorganic. Certain features of normal growth can be discovered, but many phenomena suggest unavoidably what in the field of biology would bear such names as morbid giantism, elephantiasis or metastasis.

The nature of Marian enthusiasm

It is not just simple over-abundance that is the trouble. The quantitative excess is found to be a qualitative excess also: here and there the intensity of Marian zeal is not without a certain feverishness, nor its results without exaggeration, and indeed real deviations.

We must not paint the picture too black, for, in this field, considerable progress has been made compared with the preceding three centuries in which this zeal, little enlightened by theology, seemed as if it did not know what to think up next in the threefold realm of concepts, language and practices: *Paradise Opened to Philagius by One Hundred Easy Devotions*, or another: *Kindlers of Love from the Delicious Garden of the Confraternity of the Holy Rosary*.[12] (These are the translated titles of two works published in the seventeenth century.)

The age of such poor and futureless inventions is over, but the *a-priori* tendency which encouraged an unconditional exaltation of Mary remains as vigorous as ever, compensated only by an increase in attention to detail and critical spirit. It produces many dishonest procedures in many works: texts supporting the promotion of Marian doctrine are given undue prominence, those which seem to stand in its way are either neglected or ingeniously emptied of their full weight of meaning.

To give some idea of this process it would be very significant to run through the vast literature on Genesis 3. 15, that prophetic verse full of suggestions, in which God says: "I will put enmity between you and the woman, and between your seed and her seed; it shall attack your head, and you shall attack his heel."[13]

From the fact that the contest so prophesied opposes the head of the serpent and the heel of the adversary, it is often deduced that a *perfect* victory is here prophesied, and that in the unshadowed perfection of the victory thus signified is implied for the Mother of the Descendant *par excellence*, that is to say, of the Messiah, the Immaculate Conception, the Assumption and other privileges, such as immortality. As a rule, no mention is made of another verse of Genesis which, however, obliges some change to be made in this exegesis. In 49. 16 Jacob praises Dan a being "*a serpent* in the way that bites the horse's *heels* so that his rider falls backward".[14] The serpent's attack on the heel is therefore not something which can be neglected; it signifies a real battle which the Fathers understood very well : they saw in it the power of the devil, strong to tempt Christians and to persecute them, and sometimes they also saw in it a prophecy of the death of Christ. This is only one example of what has become today an impenetrable undergrowth. We have reached the paradoxical situation in which all the mariologists see the Blessed Virgin—and sometimes all the separate theses of Marian theology —in this verse, but they arrive at this conclusion from different starting points and along different ways which are to a large extent opposed to one another. This situation makes little sense. It suggests the situation which would arise if several accountants arrived at the same total starting from different figures. They would be accused of collusion. Classical apologetics knows how to diagnose the ambiguity of such a situation when it deals with those who deny the Resurrection of Christ. Their *a-priori* agreement on the negative conclusion gives birth to a great multiplicity of divergent or contradictory theories. The unwarranted and over-elaborated exegeses poured out by the mariologists often compromise the discovery and the authority of the true riches of the theology of Mary which Scripture and Tradition deliver to us.

The source of these exaggerations is, however, perfectly honourable. A certain feeling of never quite achieving the level of the Mother of God coincides with the enthusiasm of traditional devotion in both East and West. It is surely a law in all love as in all enthusiasm to be always, in intention, a little beyond itself. It is only when it is exercised without understanding and without restraint, when it goes beyond its true territory and sets itself up as a doctrinal criterion, for example, that this enthusiasm is open to criticism. It is so, too, when it concentrates solely on its particular object, taking no account of the whole picture of which the Virgin Mary forms but a part.

The narrow specialization of Marian studies

Here we touch upon the key to the danger : specialization, which is at once a very good thing and a very bad thing.

What, in fact, is specialization? It is a process by which a precise objective is delineated so that all possible means of investigation can be concentrated on it. What results is in some ways analogous to the highlighting of an object in a spotlight, or the magnification of an object under a microscope. Some particular progress is made at the expense of a narrowing of the field of knowledge. Thus the promotion of a new order of knowledge is brought about. But this procedure is not without a double risk. For one thing, it tends to magnify the object, to exaggerate its importance, and for another, to raise it to the status of an end which will be pursued for itself, independently of anything else.

This movement towards specialization goes therefore in the opposite direction to the Wisdom movement which stands back and picks out the summits that stand out here and there in the whole expanse of vast groupings of knowledge, in order to be able to assess in a balanced way the relative importance of each separate item.

Thus, all specialization tends to become closed in: what began as sociology turns into a "sociologism" which tries to explain the whole of man (intellectual, moral and religious) by social factors alone. In the same way, the discovery of positive science gave birth to a materialism which excluded metaphysics and religion as products of bygone ages. Thus, sexology has turned into pan-sexualism. In the same way, there is a risk that mariology may become "mariologism", and Marian devotion "Marianism", or "a tendency to exalt the cult of the Virgin Mary in a way which exceeds the teaching and spirit of the Church" as it is defined in the *Nouveau Larousse illustré.*[15]

These "-isms" are characteristic of the double peril inherent in all specialization: that of becoming shut in upon itself and of encroaching in this blinkered fashion on neighbouring fields of knowledge.

Here is rediscovered in the order of scientific activity the ancestral reflex of the landowner who encloses his domains and dreams of pushing out the boundaries farther and farther, or of the conqueror fortifying his "frontiers" in the desire of pushing them ever farther out. Like the specialized sciences, mariology likes to speak of its "conquests". This vocabulary is symptomatic.

Such things do not happen without frontier incidents; sociology had (and to some extent still has) such a conflict with psychology;

psychoanalysis with psychiatry: one trying to explain everything in terms of a purely psychic origin, the other attributing
everything to purely somatic causes. Mariology has similarly
trespassed on other territories of theology, notably christology
and pneumatology.[16] There is some justification in the reproach
that the theology of the Holy Spirit has been diverted to the
advantage of the Virgin Mary.[17]

Let us analyse a little more closely what symptoms are found
to show a tendency in mariology to close in on itself and cut itself
off from the rest of theology.

(1) It has made of itself an autonomous "scientific order", an
independent discipline, based on its own special principles: a
first principle, the nature of which is under discussion, with
several theses on this point; and then secondary principles such
as the following: Mary is unique (the principle of singularity),
she surpasses other Christians in all things (principle of emi-
nence), she is in all things analogous to Christ (principle of
analogy). Whatever glory the power of God has been able to
accomplish in her, has been accomplished (principle of suitability).

Mariologists like Fr Bonnefoy reacted against this tendency.
He tried energetically to restore recognition of the fact that
Marian theology is an integral part of theology as such, and
depends essentially on those common principles which govern
it. He protested against the tendency to make of it "a branch
artificially detached"[18] from the one single trunk. But his protest
was too much against the current of the movement to be taken
seriously. The same happened when Fr Bonnichon in 1936 suggested that the different theses of mariology should be reinte-
grated into their place in the whole corpus of dogmatic theology:
the divine maternity into the treatise on the Incarnation, the
Immaculate Conception into the treatise on Original Sin, the part
of Mary in salvation into that on Redemption, the Assumption
into the treatise on the Last Things, and so on.[19] The legitimacy
of treatises gathering together all doctrine relative to Mary is
not in question. I myself am in a very bad position to suggest
any doubt about them since I have written such a treatise. But
it matters a great deal that Marian theology should, for one
thing, maintain a more positive contact with the whole of dogma,

and, for another, avoid a closed systematization and the facile reasoning of rationalist deduction. Fr Bonnichon's suggestion still has value as a warning against these dangers and as a cure of their result. With this end in view the experiment would be worth trying.

(2) Marian theology draws nourishment to a very large extent from its own sources. It shows a tendency to neglect certain texts and certain theological traditions concerning, for instance, the transcendence of Christ and the sufficiency of the Redeemer.

There exist, on the other hand, traditions which circulate among mariologists on a "closed circuit", completely ignored by all other theologians. There is a risk that specialization will accentuate this phenomenon. However useful the establishment of Marian libraries may be, they are like the tool which may become master of the man. What is found there is exclusively Marian literature. Ancient and fundamental sources, in which the Blessed Virgin figures in perspective, are little represented in them. Thus the process of specialization and the particular trends which it involves tend to be progressively exaggerated.

(3) In a similar way certain theses have a very esoteric career in Marian *milieux*. The following are not all equally widespread or well known and belong to different levels, as is obvious, but they are worth mentioning: that Mary was exempt, not only from every stain of original sin, but from any "debt" either proximate or remote; in other words, her descent from Adam brought with it no reason why she should contract this sin; that she had from her mother's womb the power of exercising intellectual cognition; that she enjoyed, frequently, or even habitually, the beatific vision; that she merited redemption *de condigno*, that is to say in justice and sufficiently; that she is secondary or associated head (*concaput*) of the mystical body; that she received the first appearance of the Risen Christ; that she exercises a certain mission jointly with that of her Son in respect of the Holy Spirit; that the reality of her appearance at Lourdes binds strictly in faith by reason of the authority of the documents of the magisterium.

Because such theses are current, largely unchallenged among mariologists, there is a tendency for them to take peaceful possession, to be treated as traditional and to become commonly accepted. Other theologians ignore them, or treat them as gratuitous, vain or extravagant, as the case may be. Their failure to intervene is due partly to their not thinking such matters worthy of their attention, and partly to fear of the trouble they would risk pulling down upon themselves from quarters which appear to be extremely susceptible and belligerent.

(4) At a deeper level mariologists tend to reinterpret in their own way the theological ideas which they take over.

For example, the force of the concept of Redemption used by theologians in the tract *De Redemptione* is somehow toned down, if not actually obscured, by the majority of mariologists who treat of the co-redemption. They usually see Redemption as *a thing* established between Christ and ourselves, which Mary merited, or even produced, in common with Christ. An authentic theology will maintain, on the contrary, as a fundamental truth and insight that Christ himself is our Redemption, just as he is "the way, the truth and the life", just as he is mediation in his own person as God–Man, *faciens utraque unum*. Seen from this angle certain obvious facts force themselves upon us: Christ alone is God, and the Blessed Virgin is not. He alone died for us, and he alone had the power to dispose of his own life with sovereign autonomy.[20] He alone rose from the dead with a divine power which is proper to him (John 2. 19), and all others, including the Virgin Mary, rise again through him. Far too often the mariologists seem to relegate these primary truths to second place and to concentrate on minor metaphorical notions, which give them room to gather under the same concepts and the same terms the roles of Christ and Mary.

The same could be said in the matter of grace. The fundamental truth in this matter is that grace is first of all the efficacious loving-kindness and the immediate presence of Almighty God, and, very specially, of the Redeeming Christ. Created grace in us is nothing but the factual, created foundation, the other face of uncreated grace; that is to say, of that presence of God as a friend who *actualizes* in us his own divine life. The notion of "grace" used in mariology reifies to excess this created grace. It is made, as it were, a thing in itself, with its own existence independent of Christ, one might almost say, stored up beforehand in heaven, in a reservoir from which Mary can draw. Here again theology is built around metaphors which leave the field open for all kinds of speculation.

In a similar way mariologists use the idea of *hypostatic order* rather than that of *hypostatic union*. The hypostatic union is the most exclusive and incommunicable element in the mystery of Christ: the *personal* union of his humanity to the Word in which it subsists. The notion of hypostatic order encompasses, on the other hand, everything that is involved in this union, and therefore the divine maternity which depends intrinsically on the person of the Word. Fr Nicolas formulated this idea in exact and unequivocal terms. In this form, the theme represents an enlightening variation on the title *Theotokos*. But other mariologists find Fr Nicolas's explanations insufficient, and make every effort to give them a stronger meaning by attributing to Mary an instrumental causality in the hypostatic union itself. In short, there is a clear tendency for the process of assimilation to continue its conquests. The idea we have discussed here is sufficiently technical not to spread outside circles in which enough care will be taken to treat it with the reserve it demands. What is more to the point is the general tendency to be seen at work in this case as in the preceding. This drawing back from the most obvious idea, and manufacturing to one's own requirements an idea which can be applied to Mary at the same time as to Christ, exhibits a tendency to obscure both the transcendence of the Word and the classical concepts which are being so subtly used. Beyond a certain point this subtlety becomes unhealthy. Nothing does a greater disservice to scholastic theology than to use it in a paradoxical fashion for special ends without reference to the great intuitions of the Faith.

(5) In the end these converging examples set before us the following question: Does the development of mariology sufficiently respect the standard of homogeneity which is so fundamental in the subject? Thirty years ago the term "evolution" applied to dogmas was suspect, and not without reason since in its usual sense it indicates heterogeneous change in animal or vegetable species which gives birth to new, quite different, species. Scholars hardly dared use even the word "development", although this showed the homogeneity better. It was still remembered that at the beginning of the century Tixeront had got into difficulties because he had called one of his books "A *History of Dogmas*" (for could immutable dogmas have a history?). Today "evolution" has a place of honour among mariologists.

Its promotion or acceleration is even quoted on occasions as the supreme object of mariology. This again is symptomatic.

While on this subject, it could be asked whether the attacks against the notion of the *debitum peccati*, irritating because reifying, have not gone so far that they compromise the fundamental dogmatic truth contained in the definition of the Immaculate Conception : that Mary was redeemed by Christ.

Similarly the thesis (which happily seems to have had very limited popularity) according to which the Blessed Virgin would be the "associated or secondary head" of the mystical body, represents a perversion of doctrine in so far as it introduces a duality into the very head of the mystical body on the symbolic as well as on the theological level: St Paul and all subsequent Christian theology are so insistent on the essential unity which must exist here. All efforts to say that the two together, Christ and Mary, form one single head will not suffice to wipe out the repulsiveness of this idea

A thesis of the same kind which is very significant is that of the co-redemptive merit *de condigno*. First hinted at in the seventeenth century by Martinez de Ripalda and Thomas Francis Urrutigoyti, and propagated in the eighteenth by Carlos del Moral, a Spanish Franciscan, it had no following[21] and was quickly forgotten. It reappeared just after the First World War, timidly and sporadically at first, was introduced forcefully at the International Marian Congress in 1950, brilliantly defended in the course of a homeric debate, and subsequently successfully spread abroad. It has thus gained so much ground in Marian circles that a recent *status quaestionis* favours considering it the predominant view.[22] Up till now theological language has differentiated very explicitly between the merit of Christ and that of Mary. He alone merited redemption *de condigno*, that is to say sufficiently and according to justice, and the Virgin Mary, completely subordinate, only merited it *de congruo*, that is to say by a merit of suitability, in the name of a gratuitous friendship not of a requirement of justice. Indeed this latter thesis had received a kind of official consecration since Pius X adopted it in his Encyclical *Ad diem illum*.[23] The Marian "conquest" which has turned the merit *de congruo* propounded by Pius X into merit *de condigno* looks very much like a revolution from the historical, as well as from the theological point of view.

Historically the thesis of merit *de congruo* was introduced for the first time by Suarez at the end of the sixteenth century. Although it seems so modest today, its promoters felt that the thesis they were advancing was very daring: "*Audacter dixi*" was still the phrase used by Salazar, a by no means timid Spanish mariologist. (It was he who in 1618 was the first to extend merit *de congruo* to the whole of Salvation.)[24] What is more, Suarez, who opened the way for this doctrine, implicitly excluded, as *contrary to faith*, the attribution of merit *de condigno* to Mary in this question.[25] This exclusion is insisted upon repeatedly in the formulations of his immediate successors, beginning with Salazar.[26] A doctrinal evolution which makes what was originally a daring thesis now seem timid, and puts in its place the thesis which was at first held to be heretical, bears all the characteristics of heterogeneous evolution.

Dogmatically, a similar sort of revolution is to be noted. According to classical mariology only Christ merited the Redemption in a sufficient manner; the merit of the Virgin Mary was seen as an addition—"an accidental excess of sweetness", as certain authors tried to define it. According to the new view, Mary merited quite sufficiently Redemption itself: her merit equals in justice the price of our sins and of our salvation, and now it is the merit of Christ which appears as a surplus addition.

Such a rapid survey as this certainly runs the risk of caricaturing the thesis in question. The efforts made by its promoters to show clearly and insistently the total subordination of Mary to Christ must be recognized. Granted this, the case is none the less a significant example of the problems set by a certain kind of development in Marian doctrine.

This collection of facts is not intended as an indictment of mariology and the mariologists (I am one myself). It does not deny either the value, the scientific nature, or the healthy perspectives of much work, or the real steps forward which have been taken in the last few years. Its only concern is to show that a problem does exist, a problem of which all mariologists owe it to themselves to be conscious. A ditch has been dug between mariology and theology. The former has developed to a large extent in a world of its own. The result is that there exist between these two disciplines such mutual ignorance, such divergences and at times hostility that there is need of a kind of ecumenism *ad intra*. There is, of course, no question of doubting the adherence to Catholic dogma of both sides, for this is without reserve. But *psychologically* the viewpoints, the mentalities, the methods, the language and the received doctrines are so different that it is not noticeably less difficult to establish a true dialogue between these Catholics with their different outlooks than it is between theologians of different denominations. One of the difficulties is the attitude of disinterest which too many theologians show towards mariology.

An analogous situation is revealed in the field of devotion. There exists today in certain quarters a tension between christocentric and mariocentric piety. Certain blinkered forms of the latter tend to act for all practical purposes as if the Virgin Mary, or even the message of a single apparition, was held to be "the means of salvation". At the other extreme, certain deeply committed Catholic Action and missionary circles give Mary no effective place at all. A priest very well placed to judge of such things wrote to me recently:

> We are witnessing a rather disturbing phenomenon: the live section of French Christianity, especially those priests who are most involved in evangelistic work, are reducing the Marian aspect of Christian spirituality to a minimum in their life as in their thought; whilst those who constitute the least lively and most superstitious section give a repulsive display of their attachment to the Mother of God. This must be looked into if the rising generation is really to live the doctrine of Ephesus.

There exists a tension between a piety which is wholly concerned with our Lady, and one which is not. To come down to facts, there are people, societies, movements, associations, books, sermons and so on which are "Marian" and others which are not; a Marian sector where she tends to be the measure of all things, and a sector where she is neglected. The attitude of each side to the other is like that of unfriendly neighbours who have found a *modus vivendi*. They alternate between the extremes of ignoring each other and outbursts latent with hostility or reproach. Where this danger is most rife, it sets off a chain reaction which becomes very intense indeed: the turning, in practice, of Marian devotion into a Marian religion leads on the other side to a religion without Mary. To be sure this extreme is reached by neither side, save perhaps by a few abnormal individuals, for the Church is always there to modify these tendencies.

Nevertheless, the problem is in the air. The press, always hungry for sensational news, has cashed in on it. Recently, a magazine with a large circulation carried in large print across its cover: "In the Catholic Church the Virgin Mary is in disgrace. Her messages are stifled. . . . Who are the men responsible? Protestants turn towards the Virgin Mary." The headline inside was worded even more harshly: "French Bishops Betray the Virgin Mary." Beneath these sensational headlines a religion was presented which was made up of practically nothing but the recent apparitions (limited almost exclusively to Fatima), about which the bishops were made to seem lukewarm and embarrassed. That such a presentation is artificial, even absurd, that the drama is invented to air political rather than religious quarrels, is clear to the informed reader. But if the subject was such as to tempt a talented journalist, if it could find a public to read it, if it formed the leading article on which the success of that particular issue depended, it was because it touched on a psychological reality, and the embryo of an evil which must be avoided at all costs: the tendency of a certain kind of Marian piety to go to extremes and then to set itself up as the judge and assessor of the Catholic faith provoking the inevitable negative reactions among those of opposite views. The hierarchy must make every effort to moderate such excesses and reintegrate this unhealthy piety in the general Catholic framework.

To point out symptoms without *ipso facto* throwing them into excessive relief, to make a clinical report without systematizing the illness and, in doing so, risking exaggeration, is a difficult thing. The reader will realize that he must be watchful against such exaggerated impressions and unjustified depreciations. What is the distribution, the exact degree attained by the excesses and misrepresentations we have noticed? Is there here a normal tension corresponding to a crisis which has arisen spontaneously, or is there the menace of a grave crisis either close at hand or distant? The second chapter of this work will attempt to throw light on these questions. The sole object of the first was to illustrate the *existence* of the problem, which can be summed up as follows: There is no doubt that the Marian move-

27

ment is fruitful, fertile and prosperous, but would it not be true to say that its abundance is excessive, its intensity unhealthy, and its development specialized and partly pathological? If something of the sort is true, should it not be remedied both for the good of Catholic theology and for the honour of the Virgin Mary?

II

An Historical Survey

HISTORY is the key to life, and anyone who knows how to gather its secrets will find the key to many of today's problems, their meaning and the direction in which they are developing.

In the preceding chapter two facts became clear: the first, that a Marian movement exists today; and the second, that the Virgin Mary is in some way a sign of contradiction. The origin of these facts must be determined. From when do they date? How did they appear? What caused them? Having established these details it will be possible to decide to what extent and in what way the first of the above facts, which in itself is normal, and the second, which is obviously very abnormal, are linked, if indeed they are. In the process the remedies for such a situation should appear.

Nature and place of the Marian movement

"The Marian movement" is a recently coined expression. If, to suppose the impossible, it had been pronounced in the presence of one of the Fathers of the Church, or of St Thomas Aquinas . . . or even several centuries later, it would have baffled them. Each of the words presents its own special difficulty.

First of all the adjective "Marian"—a word of recent appearance. A Latin noun *Mariale*, meaning an anthology of compositions in honour of the Virgin Mary, appeared in the twelfth century and in its English form "Marial" is noted by the *Oxford English Dictionary* in this meaning in 1622. But I have never met an adjective earlier than the seventeenth century, when the form was *marianus*, and in English "Marian" (*O.E.D.*, 1701). Whatever its exact date may be, the use of this epithet is a sign of the times. It was created to indicate the recent phenomenon not merely of a specialization, but of a polarization. Lively devotion to the Virgin Mary already existed, but the question was never asked whether such a person or such a form of prayer was "more" or "less" Marian, even less whether it was "Marian" or not.

Supposing a theologian from early times had come across this phrase, he would have asked how, when it has to do with the Virgin Mary, an object of dogmatic truth, there can be talk of a *movement*.

What then is a "movement"? The concept, if not the fact it represents, is recent in origin and has wide currency today. The *Oxford English Dictionary* defines the word as "a series of actions and endeavours by a body of persons, tending more or less continuously towards some special end", and dates the use of the word in this sense from 1828 as, for example, in *the Labour Movement*. Applied in this sense, the word "movement" denotes a sociological phenomenon characterized not merely by change but by the promotion of some particular object. The meaning behind "movement" adds to the notion of a tendency in human society the further notions of self-awareness and of a certain organic concept coextensive with this awareness. Organic concept rather than organization, because even before the existence of an external organization, a movement implies some kind of convergence which shows itself quite spontaneously in groups with related ideals and aims. It answers in fact to a deep and often irrepressible need. Were this not the case, the special word "movement" would not be used.

Whatever the lexicographical problem presented by the word, our age of change and accelerated socialization is characterized by a multiplicity of movements in all kinds of spheres—emancipation movements, revolutionary movements, ideological movements, even artistic movements such as surrealism.

In the Church itself we have a liturgical movement, a biblical movement, an ecumenical movement, a missionary movement, and to these perhaps there might be added an ecclesiological movement. Obviously each is concerned with an object of faith, and because of this the practical and theoretical orders are inseparably involved in it. In addition, all these movements present two aspects—scholarly study and pastoral activity.

Such movements existing within the Church raise certain problems. To speak of movement is to speak of change. Furthermore, outside the domain of religion, such movements usually have a revolutionary character, as consideration of the examples quoted above will show. The Church is a society based on tradition. No true revolution could possibly affect its dogma and its fundamental structure—what it holds from the beginning, from its Founder. There is no place for the word revolution in the Church. It could be applied only in an attenuated sense as meaning rapid spectacular change, or in a clearly delineated sense to mean the effort by which the Church "reforms itself in its head and its members" on earth, as the medieval expression had it. The fact is that, if the Church, inasmuch as it is an institution ordained from above, transcends the vicissitudes of this earth, there is produced within it a permanent *revolution*: but this exists in the conversion of sinners who become members of, or who return to, this indefectible society. For the two words, revolution and conversion, have the same meaning—the act of turning one's back on one's former outlook. But the revolution that is a conversion is, precisely, an adhesion to what is most essential and permanent in the Church. In matters of fundamentals only those movements are acceptable which introduce *homogeneous* changes and, moreover, changes which are intended to reinforce this homogeneity.

Here we are touching on the delicate situation of "movements" in the Church. Their proper nature as movements should lead them to take on a revolutionary form. Even if this temptation is not surrendered to, the fact that they are attacking abuses and recommending changes lays them open to mistrust and suspicion. It is not just faint-heartedness which is the cause of this; every innovation (even if proposed as a restoration) brings with it risks of exaggeration, deviation, over-eagerness, and, at the very worst, heresy or schism. Therefore, it is the lot of every movement to awaken the vigilance of the Church and to undergo in a certain degree both interior and exterior crises.

The liturgical movement took a long time to achieve the official position it holds in the Church today. It caused considerable disquiet and called forth official warnings. It was suspected of wishing to ascribe to the priesthood of the faithful, of which it sought to restore both the idea and the exercise, a role in the consecration of the Eucharist necessary to its validity. For a time it was a question whether the Holy See would not condemn the movement outright. What actually happened is that

Pius XII published a very positive encyclical, in which constructive elements and encouraging directives took priority over such
reservations as certain momentary and limited excesses made
necessary. Since then the movement has taken root in Rome
itself. Between its promoters and the Congregation of Rites has
sprung up a fruitful collaboration. In this way were undertaken
the great reforms, which began with the restoration of the Holy
Week liturgy (1951-5) and, later, took on the breadth that we
have seen in the Council. This last stage was arduous. The liturgical *schema* appeared daring, and there were fears that it might
be rejected. In actual fact, the final vote was all but unanimous,
with 97 per cent of the votes in its favour. The movement today
is already bearing an abundant harvest of fruits which have
become indistinguishably the fruits of the whole Church. One
of the great successes of the century has been to channel the
movement and to integrate it institutionally.

The history of the ecumenical movement has been still more
eventful. Between the two wars the pioneers worked amidst
difficulties, threats and suspicion from all sides that kept on
reappearing over the years. It was a depressing test but one not
without fruit in so delicate a matter, where so many snares lay
in the way. Then, suddenly, there came the pontificate of John
XXIII and with it the movement emerged into the light. The men
who had worked in the shadows with nothing but a long-term
hope have become the hard-working mainstays of the Secretariat
for Unity, which has promoted the ecumenical dialogue and
succeeded in getting Protestant and Orthodox observers invited
to the Council.

As for the biblical movement—the oldest of all—it seemed to
have emerged from its limbo with *Divino Afflante* (1943). Recent
events have shown, however, that it has not yet completely freed
itself from the quicksands of its difficulties.

So let no one be scandalized if we have put forward some
critical problems concerning the Marian movement. Risks are
implicit in every movement, and its spirit could not be fulfilled
completely and truly unless it were subjected to some element of
criticism and testing. Authorized criticism is certainly the province of the teaching authority, but this does not make it any
the less desirable that the members of the movement should
themselves forestall or reduce its excesses, and thus dispense

authority from any need to intervene in a negative fashion or to show its disapproval.

Every movement has its difficulties and its risks, but the positive element, which is the most important, must not be lost sight of. The movements in the Church demonstrate its prophetic function, a function in which every member takes his part in his own way, and which is one of the factors in its ability to adapt itself to the times, an adaptation which is made all the more necessary by the ever more rapid evolution of the world at the present time. In more precise terms, in such movements can be found a proof of the existence of a capacity for cleansing, restoration, revivification, and spiritual reawakening in which the vitality of the Church and the spread of its influence are confirmed.

It is only necessary to recall the position of the Bible in the life of the Catholic Church thirty years ago. Not only was it neglected, but the opinion was still current in certain Catholic circles that the Old Testament (or even the whole Bible) was on the Index. When I was young, I heard this opinion repeated even by priests. Only a little more recently the papers, even the Catholic ones, reported without the slightest upset the words of an over-enthusiastic convert who throwing a dagger and a "Protestant Bible" at the feet of Pius XII said: "This is the weapon with which I wanted to kill you, and the book in which I learnt my false teaching." At that time the publishing of Catholic Bibles was at a very low ebb, in sharp contrast with the position among Protestants. What a long way we have come!

At about the same time the liturgical situation was little happier. In a justly famous Catholic university just before the 1939 war, a professor had dared to suggest that the liturgy should be restored to due honour. His colleagues thought he was joking; they laughed! "Liturgy" was to their minds a synonym of "rubrics". A liturgist was one of those men who traced the strange history of the maniple, and wrote a commentary on the reply of the Congregation of Rites defining that when the hands are joined it is correct for the right thumb to be crossed over the left. Such were then the decisions that were requested from Rome under the guise of progress. Today the true riches of the liturgy have been revealed so that it can be ignored no longer. The result has been a fruitful transformation.

And how many prejudices concerning the ecumenical movement have been swept away in the last few years (1959-63), and what a change in the mental and spiritual atmosphere has been the result! We are still certainly far from a solution, and in this field it is essential not to live on illusions; but one of the fruits of this movement has been to bring into being a method of dialogue in which clarity and truth can stand at the very roots of charity.

These reflexions cannot but cause some perplexity to discerning readers. Is it possible to classify under the same heading the movements which we have just examined, and the Marian movement which was the subject of the previous chapter?

It will be found that although all these movements correspond to the general definition which was given (an organic social phenomenon characterized by the promotion of a particular object), there appear between them both correlations and contrasts which point to a division into distinct groups: the Eucharistic and Marian on the one hand; the biblical, liturgical, missionary, and even the ecclesiological movements on the other.

The correlations are obvious. The Marian Congresses which are an advance sign of the rise of the Marian movement were born of the Eucharistic Congresses and in direct imitation of them.

The fact that the movements in the second group are similar, encourage one another and spontaneously lend one another strength and support is even more weighty and obvious evidence. The missionary and ecclesiological movements are both sustained by the general return to the Bible, and the progress made in the biblical movement has of itself brought about an ecumenical *rapprochement*, etc.

On the other hand, the orientations of the two groups are in some ways divergent. The chief characteristic of the first is the promotion of a devotional objective, of the second a spontaneous concern for renewal.

The inspiration of these last is of recent date, but the first two go back to the seventeenth century when the Eucharist and the Virgin Mary aroused great zeal and an unprecedented outburst of fresh action.

This discovery at once reveals the roots of both types of movement.

34

The more recent group (biblical, liturgical, ecumenical) springs from a deep and unpremeditated need to restore those truths and those attitudes which had been neglected in the blaze of anti-Protestant polemics. It is one of the unfortunate results of every kind of polemic, as of every war, that it gives an excessive importance to the threatened areas while allowing the essential and vital values, which are not menaced, to be forgotten. Armed conflict brings with it the neglect of agriculture and civilized existence. A country at war is emptied of its substance in order to strengthen its defences. Because the Reformers belittled the visible and hierarchical aspects of the Church, retaining only the interior and mystical ones, the Counter-Reformation in its less enlightened forms tended to neglect this essential factor and to limit ecclesiology to a kind of "hierarchology", or, in extreme cases, to a treatise on the Holy See. Because the Protestants put the Bible in an exclusive position, the tendency was to push it into the background. Because the Protestants gave great value to faith and little to rite, the tendency was to fall back on a formal ritualism in which the role of faith was obscured. In short, the unquestionable zeal expended in the service of anti-Protestant apologetic had as its other side the neglect into which important values of faith were allowed to fall. The ecclesiological, biblical and liturgical movements are restoring to their rightful place the traditional values which were hidden in the fires of the Counter-Reformation combats. The ecumenical movement is restoring a dialogue destined to discover a basis in common values, and to enlarge this by a common return to the sources. Thus, this return to the sources is the essential methodological starting-point for all these movements.

The Eucharistic and mariological movements (and, in a certain sense, the "josephological" movement which has come from it and is a division of it) took shape, on the other hand, in the main stream of the Counter-Reformation. The stimulus which gave them shape as movements came from a will to make reparation for the insult done to the Blessed Sacrament and the Virgin Mary by the Reformers.

It is because of this that the Eucharistic movement insisted so forcibly on the Real Presence as such, for this was the chief point queried by Protestantism. From this springs the one-sided growth of the cult: ever more numerous and more solemn services of

Benediction, perpetual Exposition, and Mass before the Blessed Sacrament exposed, a thing unknown before that time.

In a similar way, the desire to avenge the honour of the Blessed Virgin, to reinstate her in her rightful high place, to find new jewels for her crown (a preoccupation for which one would search in vain—in these terms—at any earlier date), to consecrate her privileges by solemn definitions—all these are the dominant characteristics of the Marian movement which gradually took shape in the Church from the beginning of the seventeenth century.

For this reason, it is not difficult to understand why for so long the Eucharistic and Marian movements have remained apart from the liturgical and biblical movements, nor why they have so often displayed aims diametrically opposed to these other movements when, by their object and their specifically "Church" vocation, they ought normally to be of one mind with them. It springs from the fact that, on one side, the orientation is that of the Counter-Reformation, and, on the other, one which is seeking to compensate for it.

This is the explanation for facts such as the following: Marian treatises of even a very recent date have given but a minor, and indeed, an utterly negligible place, to the liturgy. This, the principal and normative dimension in the prayer-life of the Church, is mentioned in them as one type of devotion among others. In the same way, the attempts on the part of the mariologists to get new Marian feasts or invocations introduced often go completely counter to the effort which is being made to clear the liturgy of recently introduced feasts in order to restore to it its main lines, its true proportions and its meaning.

The fact that the Marian movement has for so long dissociated itself from exegesis can be explained in a similar way—whether it be downright neglect of the Bible or use of it employing facile methods out of keeping with the accepted standards of scientific hermeneutics. To a large extent mariology remains the domain of the "plenary" or "accommodated" sense. Even the first of these is scarcely accepted *in practice* among biblical scholars. I put the following question to someone who had written an article on just this subject: "Could you quote any examples of the use of the plenary sense outside the field of the Marian question?" After a moment's reflexion he assured me that he could find none. The development of Marian dogma has posed this problem of the plenary sense and such interpretation is scarcely in favour with specialists in exegesis.

Although they seem to have taken us far from our subject, the above analyses and examples bring out some interesting lessons:

(1) One of the conditions for the fruitfulness of any movement is that it must not exist on isolated specialities, even less on esoteric currents of thought, but must answer to the essential needs of the life of the Church. If not, it will be reduced to maintaining itself artificially through the expedients of pettifogging manoeuvres, outside publicity and appeals to the official support of authority. It is then nothing more than the skeleton or the caricature of a movement. This can surely throw light on the conduct of the Marian movement.

(2) The ambiguity that always surrounds any movement invites us to underline a distinction which John XXIII proposed recently in *Pacem in Terris* on the subject of Marxism, it was said, but with a meaning that can be taken quite generally—the distinction between *doctrine* and *movement*: "A doctrine, once it is fixed and formulated, does not change any further, whereas movements [are subject to] evolution."

This distinction applies just as much to movements within the Church, but not without a shift of meaning, for here (and this is a fundamental difference from Marxism) revealed *doctrine* held by the Church from above for all time until the consummation of the age is the best of all its possessions: historical movements which affect it must be assessed by reference to this essential element. Their effective purpose is to assure a better formulation, a formulation better adapted to the times, a fuller or more explicit formulation of the doctrine of Jesus Christ, and also to procure its realization in the lives of men. But if a movement can give rise to an effort for the clarification of a dogma (as, in a complementary way, such a clarification can well give rise to a movement), it can also be the starting-point of corruption in dogma, that is, of heresy. In short, the doctrine of Christ (and its dogmatic formulation) is certain, but movements are subject to error. The doctrine is irreformable, and the movements connected with it are transitory. The doctrine is pure, the movements not necessarily so. The doctrine has absolute value, movements only relative value. Once they have achieved their end, they lose their nature and their *raison d'être* as "move-ments".

The connection between the two can be made clearer by com-paring a movement to the more rapid currents which form in a river when it passes through narrow places—under the arch of a bridge for example, or through a breach in a weir. The stream at this point may be moving much more quickly than elsewhere, but the sheet of water that surrounds it downstream is almost motionless; there, in fact, counter-currents are set up in reaction. The river has a troubled, disturbed look, with all the attendant noise, eddies and foam. We may compare this current to a "move-ment", but the whole river to the life of faith and charity which is the life of the Church. The current is not the river. Its function could be said to be : to help the stream catch up on a delay in its flow. It is limited in width as well as in length. It is but an episode in the whole life of the river, destined to lose itself sooner or later in the normal peaceful progress and smooth flow of the main stream. In the same way, movements are not the Church. They may be necessary at certain periods in its life, certain difficult moments, times of backwardness or of trouble, but they are never an end in themselves; they are destined to mingle sooner or later in the main current of the Church's life.

As we stand on the threshold of delicate questions of a very special nature, this analysis and image are necessary in order to prevent both misunderstanding and passionate reactions.

In presenting in a critical fashion the problem of the Marian situation and the Marian movement at the present time, in undertaking a self-examination on a largish scale, it might seem that I am putting on trial the faith of the Church, if not the Virgin Mary herself. But no! It is not any dogma which is in question, nor the Church, which has the promise of eternal life and whose faith is preserved indefectibly in its essential purity by the Holy Spirit. What is in question is the historical movement of which the doctrine is the object. It falls to the theologian, according to his ability (and not by virtue of any teaching authority), to present a clear diagnosis of such phenomena, report-ing on their general state of health and any crisis that may be threatening.

In analysing that "episode" in the life of the Church which

we have found a "movement" to be, and paying attention to the good or overbold commitments which characterize it together with the frictions and oppositions resulting from it, there is a danger of our forgetting the essential part of that life. This would be a serious mistake. Whatever the glamour, whatever the spectacular character of a movement, the life of the Church carries on at all times, clear, sure, without noise, in a way which is particularly deep among those whom Malègue calls "the middle classes of sanctity" and Scripture, more simply, "the poor of Yahweh". Here lies what is essential on the level of *living*. It will never do if the eddies and splashes which are perforce the objects in the foreground of our study make us forget the river.

Should our diagnosis touch certain sensitive spots, any exaggeration—and still more, any dramatization—of the situation must be avoided. It must be looked at in the light of the Church's wayfaring state. If the Church really does guard indefectibly the essentials of the faith, it does this, not in a merely automatic or material fashion, but in a living way, subject to the hazards of freedom, the vicissitudes of our human condition. That is why it is compared with a boat which, although it cannot founder, is not sheltered from damage in the storm or from the terrors of the night. The Church keeps the truth which it possesses by its day-to-day activity of living it, teaching it and defending it; and, though what is essential remains safe, it can still be found to be menaced, clouded or obscured. Large Christian communities can be submerged, and the Church only drag itself clear of the peril *in extremis* by the success, unhoped for on a human level, of efforts which seemed condemned to be swallowed up in the current of history. We have only to think of the Arian crisis, for example, when the Church, half-enmeshed in certain postulates of Hellenic philosophy, weighed down by the ruling hand of the emperors, presented something like an appearance of semi-arianism. ("The world woke up surprised to find itself Arian," wrote St Jerome.) It was by the humble labours of apparently isolated bishops, the Cappadocians in particular, that it emerged from this dead end just at the moment at which historical determinism seemed to have caught it irresistibly in its grip. The Church did not free itself from the Nestorian, Monophysite and Monothelite controversies without active, enterprising and perilous thought; and the last of these was so serious that the Ecumenical Council of Constantinople III felt it necessary to include the deceased pope Honorius in its condemnation. Many of these crises sprang from movements of a dangerous kind whose unilateral demands vitiated an essential point of dogma.

Nothing is more certain than that the difficulties which Marian theology and piety are undergoing today are far removed from these extreme cases which we find it hard even to visualize. At the time of Nicaea they led to excommunications so frequent and so numerous that the Council decided it was worthwhile to provide for two synods a year in every province to look into disputed cases (Canon 5). In comparison with these striking examples, the position of Marian theology and piety seems clear and positive. Its essentials are fixed in a body of dogmatic definitions which are particularly numerous, and in a framework of liturgical norms and other directives which no one disputes. Here we are on solid ground. To take as the object of our analysis the options and oppositions which show themselves on this ground is not, assuredly, to contest the essential, but on the contrary, to wish to restore it to its front-rank position. This analysis of the idea of a movement was, therefore, a necessary preamble to grasping the significance of two very special questions which form the main object of this chapter. The first of them: From when does the "Marian *movement*" date?

Origin of the Marian movement

The difficulty found in answering this question has two causes. One is the relative vagueness of the concept. From what point can one speak precisely of a *movement* in preference to the idea of a *trend* or *line* of thought, which are vaguer terms, or a *school* or *fashion* which represent phenomena which, historically speaking, are much less profound? The difficulty would crop up again if, for example, we asked the question: Are positivism, romanticism, impressionism and cubism "movements"?

The other is that the twentieth-century Marian movement has its roots deep in the past. It developed in stages. At what particular moment does it formally correspond to the concept in question? The answer to this is bound to make allowance for this gradual development.

The reaching out of Christian piety towards the Virgin Mary, the deepest spring of the Marian movement, is an ancient thing. Two moments in history can be pinpointed as giving a particularly clear manifestation of its rise in the Church.

The first centres on the first dogmatic and liturgical formulations, of which the beginnings can be placed towards the end of the fourth century, the key-period around the Council of Ephesus (431), and its fruitful extensions up to the eighth century, above all in the East.

Then there is the Latin flowering, after a long preparation, manifesting itself at the end of the eleventh century, reaching its climax in the twelfth, the origin of the present movement. It is at this time that the Virgin Mary begins to be thought of, no longer only as the mother, but also as the associate of Christ, placed in a mediating position between him and the Church, endowed with a universal role in the work of salvation. At this time interest begins to be shown in her privileges considered in themselves.

For the first of these two periods both the word "Marian" and the word "movement" would be anachronistic. The place of Mary is found within the framework of the mystery of the Incarnation, so completely in reference to this mystery that the idea of praying to Mary is still unusual at the time of St Augustine.[1]

For the second phase, there is more. Nevertheless, it is only in retrospect that there is a temptation to call it a movement. The driving force has about it nothing of a concerted effort, nothing organic, let alone organized. The doctrinal enhancement occurs spontaneously in the course of sermons preached on the Marian feasts, or of commentaries on the Scriptures without any particular aim in view. Marian theology is still not organized systematically or as a specialist discipline. It remains integrated in the whole. It is very significant that a St Bernard was able to preach a sermon on the Assumption without mentioning the Blessed Virgin. If Marian piety was already being organized into confraternities, these are not yet pointed towards such objectives of promotion or defence as characterize a movement.

One would feel more tempted to speak of an "immaculatist movement" aimed at promoting the doctrine of the Immaculate Conception, and beginning in the fourteenth century. This new phenomenon appeared in the prolongation of Scotus's reaction to the "maculist" opinions of the thirteenth century. But the Church, fearing quarrels between the Franciscan and the Dominican opinions, limited the possibilities of expression and organization for this line of thought, which contains the conquering power of a movement.

In the seventeenth century we see the blossoming of a tremendous, specialized Marian literature; no one has ever catalogued it, but it runs into thousands of volumes. This literature is devoted to the promotion and defence of Marian devotion, hindered but not discouraged by the action of the Holy Office which until 1661 was just as opposed to the publication of openly "immaculatistic" books as to publications of the opposing school.[2] Marian piety is at that time very inventive. Feasts, institutions, invocations and forms of piety are multiplied. This trend was born about 1600, grew until 1650, then showed signs of flagging, was aroused here and there, particularly by polemics against it, and seemed to exhaust itself towards the end of the eighteenth century.

It was reborn about the third decade of the nineteenth century. The impetus came from an unexpected quarter : a movement coming not from below but from above. On the one hand a series of apparitions set the whole world talking—the Miraculous Medal (1830), La Salette (1846), Lourdes (1858). On the other there was the definition of the Immaculate Conception by Pius IX. But this intense spirit of enthusiasm at that time was hampered from within by the theological poverty of the period. Marian piety for want of other means of expression had to satisfy itself with the multiplication of new titles and invocations, often over-subtle or even ridiculous, against which the Holy Office had to act.[3] All the literature still depended on the authors of the seventeenth and eighteenth centuries whose works were resurrected and re-edited, their style being brought up to date. Thus it was that the *Traité* of Grignion de Montfort was discovered hidden in a chest. A few theologians did some original work, but they were isolated : Passaglia and Malou at the time of the definition; Newman and then Scheeben a little later; Terrien at the beginning of the twentieth century. To these could be added Fr Goedts, who in 1904 edited the first *ex-professo* work on the "mediation" of our Lady, a book printed privately and a fore-

runner of the sudden expansion which came at the end of the
First World War.

This is the moment, in my opinion, when the "Marian *movement*" acquired the solidity, the conscious and organic structure,
the sense of direction which make it necessary to use that word
to describe it.

In 1913 Cardinal Mercier put forward an idea. Deeply conscious of the fact of Mary's presence in the life of Christians and
of the Church, one of the dominant traits of modern Marian
devotion, he endeavoured to obtain a definition of Mary's
mediation. This activity, interrupted by the war, was taken up
again in 1921. The cardinal obtained from Pius XI the institution
of a Feast of the Mediation (granted to such dioceses as should
request it) and also the setting up of three commissions, in Rome,
Belgium and Spain, with the task of studying the definability of
the doctrine. The Spanish commission is best known for the
inquiries and monographs of Fr Bover, S.J., which appeared in
large numbers from 1923 until his death The most active commission was that in Belgium, round the cardinal. Thus a new
attitude appeared, a movement for Marian studies undertaken by
qualified theologians (generally professors at universities and
major seminaries) with the double purpose of investigating
sources and reflecting on doctrine. Marian literature, badly in
need of new, serious topics to pursue, here found an objective,
a line of approach and a field of work which was almost in-
exhaustible.

The movement grew like a snowball. From 1921 to 1926 it was
limited to articles published almost exclusively in Belgian or
Spanish reviews. Then, there appeared a series of works of which
these articles were the inspiration, and the first source of
documentation. "Mediatrix", "Christ's Associate", "Co-redemptrix", such are the key-words which appear in the titles of these
books. The idea of mediation, which up till then had played only
a very discreet part in Marian theology, now tends to become a
central theme, the unifying principle of everything which concerns the relation of Mary to men. Some were prepared to go so
far as to consider that the "first principle" of Marian theology
lay in this direction, the principle of the total partnership of
Mary with Christ.

From 1934 onwards the horizons of this research movement

widened; it spread out and was organized into stable institutions. Societies of Marian studies were founded with the aim of scrutinizing the theological bases of devotion to Mary in annual meetings: a Flemish society in 1931, a French society in 1934, a Spanish in 1940, a French-speaking Belgian, an American, Canadian and German in 1950, a Mexican in 1954, a Colombian and Polish in 1959. The development and co-ordination of these societies were stimulated by the setting up of an International Marian Academy in 1950. Through this many collected works are published, and many periodical congresses instigated. The *Acta* of these are often monumental works of twenty or so volumes for one Congress.

The definition of the Assumption and the Marian years at the end of the pontificate of Pius XII (1950, 1954, 1958) both contributed to the amplification, the actualization and the multiplication of studies, of undertakings and of manifestations of devotion.

Movements are characterized by their particular orientation. How can we define the orientation of the modern Marian movement? It is obvious that the original concern was an effort towards the promotion of certain dogmas. Centred first of all on the mediation, it refocused momentarily on the definition of the Assumption which became the catalyst to its work from 1944 to 1950.

From then two divergent orientations can be distinguished. One of them sees in the definition of the Assumption the starting-point and the exemplar for promoting a further series of privileges of Mary.[4] The mariological societies founded in Latin America, following in the wake of the Spanish society, are working along these lines. The other line of thought appeared at exactly the same date but gives shape to research and works of a new type. These proceed from the feeling that the need is not to develop and augment, but to situate Marian doctrine in its true perspective in the whole picture of dogma. This tendency takes shape round a theme which until this time had been all but absent from the productions of the Marian movement: *Mary and the Church*.

These two orientations go their separate ways, juxtaposed and not without a degree of internal tension between them. At first this was scarcely adverted to, but, even while hidden, the opposition of the two views caused some uneasiness. The ecclesio-

44

logical current, born in Germany and France, taking as its task the exact evaluation of the proportions and significance of Marian doctrine, is felt to be an unwelcome brake on the first impulse of the Marian movement, a minimizing factor, and, indeed, a subversive element tending to separate Mary from Christ in order to reduce her to the level of the Church. From such attitudes to this approach many troublesome clashes have arisen.

The joining up of the ecclesiological and Marian movements in spite of everything is an important and significant fact. It represents the coming together of two complementary currents whose vocation was to complete each other—one the offspring of the Counter-Reformation, the other of efforts to compensate for its excesses. A similar encounter, a most fruitful one, has come about at the most recent Eucharistic Congresses. This has involved the devotional movement from which the congresses originally sprang, and the liturgical movement, which, as we saw, is connected with the ecclesiological.

Recently, the pontificate of John XXIII and the Council have brought about a still more difficult confrontation, a test which the Marian movement would have been unable to bear had it not been for the contacts with ecclesiological studies in the last few years. The ecumenical dialogue has assumed a position of first-rank importance in the Church under the direct influence of the Pope himself. Marian dogma is, however, one of the biggest stumbling-blocks in this dialogue. Because of this, the Marian movement finds that it is being called on to moderate its pursual of dogmatic "conquests" and instead to sift out the true meaning of the present dogmas along the lines already set down by the ecclesiological approach.

The Marian movement is, therefore, at a moment of crisis. It is caught between the attraction of two divergent, and perhaps even opposing, factors. On the one side are its expansive and defensive instincts, on the other, the invitation to return to the sources, to find its right place in the general teaching of the Church, to ecumenism. No time has been lost in facing up to this, but it is very clear that great difficulty is being found in entering into the spirit of *dialogue* which is characteristic of this outlook. The first works which have appeared from Marian *milieux*, instead of having this character, have rather been in the nature of theoretical expositions and critical examinations of the positions of separated Christians. The Marian movement is on the threshold of a new period of testing, and there is present an obscure fear that it may be swallowed up if it should commit itself to this new, ecclesiological path. We shall return to this problem in more detail in Chapter V. Here the important thing has merely been to situate this point in its context in the present evolution of the Marian movement. It stands at a crossroads. The invitation addressed to it is to seek the way of humility and give up that of resounding triumphs.

The Virgin Mary, a source of dispute

Having thus clarified the present situation and the origins of the Marian movement, it will be relatively easy to answer the second and much more delicate question : When and where did the Virgin Mary become a source of dispute within Catholicism?

Here again we must distinguish between momentary, transitory conflicts and an habitual state of tension. Under this latter aspect, analysed in the preceding chapter, the phenomenon is limited to the West and seems to be unknown in the East. Within Western Christendom it is of relatively recent occurrence.

The doctrinal conflicts of the patristic period in which the Virgin Mary was involved are now no longer subjects of dispute. The difficulties which arose concerning such things as the holiness of Mary, different aspects of her virginity or her divine motherhood, were rapidly and unanimously resolved in the fourth and fifth centuries without leaving any trace of uneasiness. Such conflicts, which we today may tend to think of as "Marian", were then seen in an essentially christological perspective. Thus, as an example, the virginity of Mary was seen primarily as the most specific sign of the Incarnation.

Does Ephesus offer much more than that? According to the legend which sees in Cyril the noble knight sworn to the service of the Theotokos, set against a Nestorius who insults her, it does. The Council of Ephesus was certainly concerned with devotion to Mary; it was the occasion of fresh insights in this respect; the slights of Nestorius against the title of Theotokos certainly aroused indignation; but the person of the Virgin Mary in itself was not the formal object of the quarrel. This essentially concerned the communication of the properties, the attribution to the Son of God, eternal and impassible, of what came to him through the flesh—in particular, birth, passion and death. If Nestorius, for this reason, came to challenge the already traditional title of Theotokos, he did not insist on this point and very soon gave it up as a line of argument. As far as the honour and the title of the Virgin Mary were concerned, unanimity was, for all practical purposes, complete before the Council, and this was one of the reasons why it was not felt necessary to go on to any definition or formal condemnation on this point, as Cyril had recommended in the very first of his anathematisms. What is more, Cyril's own works contain, as concerns Mary's holiness, ideas which today we should find scarcely less shocking than those of Nestorius, but which then provoked no reaction and presented no difficulty.[5] Whatever may be the truth about the details of the story, so difficult to disengage from retrospective interpretations of the facts, the subject of the disputes of Ephesus was certainly not the Virgin Mary but the communication of the properties, of which the title Mother of God was but a particular instance.

Similarly in the ninth century, the dispute between Radbertus and Ratramnus over the nature of the virginity *in partu* was brief and produced immediate agreement as to the virginal integrity of Mary. In contrast, Radbertus's warning against the *bodily* Assumption which he judged suspect because of its apocryphal sources, did not arouse any lively reaction. The Latin world in general accepted without difficulty not to go beyond belief in the assumption of Mary's soul, and for three centuries more did not concern itself with any disputes as to what happened to her body; but for a few unobtrusive exceptions it did not even ask the question! It is true that Radbertus's warning was given under the powerful pseudonym of St Jerome and in a very positive context, but other times would not have accepted so easily such a brake on the development of a "pious belief". A violent argument would have erupted.

It was quite definitely the prolonged controversy over the Immaculate Conception that little by little created an atmosphere of crisis which split the theologians into opposed camps and initiated the contentious situation in which Marian theology has since existed.

Nothing of this is yet to be seen in the conflict between St Bernard and the canons of Lyons. The canons had instituted in 1138 the Feast of the Conception, which had recently arrived in England from the East and won ground rapidly on the Continent from the second decade of the twelfth century. St Bernard reproaches them for making an innovation in respect of a theological object which he judges to be erroneous. But his reproof began no large-scale conflicts.[6]

Nor are any open disputes to be found in the course of the thirteenth century, in which the great majority of scholars took up a position—with various nuances—favouring the idea of a purification and sanctification posterior to the conception. As for Scotus, his reaction against the common opinion (which his master William de Ware and Raymond Lull were almost alone in not sharing) was so modest in its conclusions, which show firmly the *possibility* of the privilege of the Immaculate Conception and more discreetly its suitability, that in his own lifetime his decisive action suffered no violent attack. This prudence is the least known of his merits, but not, for that reason, the least of them or the least fruitful. Later, the fervour of Scotus's supporters obscured this aspect so that they were able to attribute to him a spectacular victory over his adversaries won in the course of a solemn university disputation. But that is pure legend, as has now been established.[7]

In the fourteenth and fifteenth centuries, the controversy developed, and the "immaculatist" thesis became more widespread, to the extent that the Council of Basle inquired into it with a view to defining it, and did in fact define it, but at a time when the Council had become schismatic.[8] At Basle, the discussions seem to have remained courteous and peaceful. It was at the end of the fifteenth century that the debate became more bitter, and emerged into the market-place. It appeared in public sermons, so that the Holy See had to intervene to restore peace. Sixtus IV forbad either party to call the other opinion heretical under pain of excommunication. This measure failed to check the bitterness of the debates. In the sixteenth century and in the seventeenth, the popes had to take more radical measures forbidding all discussion of the subject—measures which were always circumvented. The violence of the quarrel, hampered but not suppressed by the pontifical decrees, was to rage in a state of almost indescribable confusion.[9] Nevertheless, the "maculists" showed no disaffection towards the Virgin Mary, but rather the contrary.

A second factor interfered in this situation: the Protestant crisis occurred in a time of decadence. Theology was ravaged by Nominalism. Devotion to the Virgin Mary had been made insipid by sentimentality, had been corrupted by superstitious infiltrations, and rendered ridiculous by the inventions of credulity (collections of false miracles and vain promises of cheap salvation). It was the time of coy, simpering Virgins and generally of an art which, having lost the sense of the sacred, made of the Virgin Mary nothing more than a naturally beautiful woman. For their models artists went less to Christian tradition than to the beauties of the day—choosing them even among courtesans. These abuses stirred up the anti-Marian reaction of the Reformers. Their opposition was contained within the logic of their fundamental principles, but it could have allowed the retention of the essential dogmas which had developed up to that time, together with the basic attitude of devotion. All this lasted for many years with Luther, in part until his death. A significant indication of the source of his gradual disaffection can be seen in this declaration dating from 1523: "I desire that the cult of Mary be totally abandoned solely because of the abuses which arise from it."[10]

Here we observe two phenomena which were to be decisive in all the future development.

Devotion which is an abuse and to a great extent superstitious appears as a caricature; it provokes disaffection. Through it, the face of which it presents a distorted image comes to be despised, if not hated. In the same way as certain pharisaical forms of Catholicism provoke a hatred of Christ among those who do not know him, so certain aberrations in Marian devotion cause the Virgin Mary herself to be despised.

This contempt and hostility give rise to a contrary phenomenon. The devotees of Mary are roused to indignation, and their indignation soon adds to their zeal an aggressive and passionate element which lends a kind of support to the very abuses which all should be trying to outgrow. So the two processes stir each other up and lead towards open conflict.

The two reactions obviously cannot be placed on the same footing. The first may be provoked by errors, but it follows a

D   49

mistaken course, not only because of the lack of charity shown towards the erring devotees, but objectively, and in grave matter, in that, because of the abuses of devotion, the devotion itself is rejected; because of excrescences of doctrine, the doctrine itself is denied. Reaction against dogmatic error is essential to the integrity of the faith.

Once this difference has been made perfectly clear, it must be recognized that psychologically polemics and the passionate attitudes which are involved in them cause, on both sides, similar casualties.

First they lead to narrow-mindedness. In controversial discussion openness to the fullness of truth is always restricted, and each side falls into its own particular forms of exaggeration.

Suspicion always arises too, for every quarrel creates the fear of plot and conspiracy. Every witchhunt ends up by inventing witches to hunt. Thus the Jansenists, whose Marian devotion was originally irreproachable and like a twin-brother to that practised by the French School, were considered later to be secret enemies of the Virgin Mary. On them responsibility was placed for the lukewarmness and the attacks occasioned by certain abuses in Marian devotion. This is what forced them into that attitude of disaffection towards Mary which was a very late and narrowly circumscribed phenomenon in Jansenism.[11]

Aggressiveness appears: when war has been declared on the psychological level, even if it is a holy war, lack of understanding and positive hatred always do their evil work in some way. A charitable attitude, constructive dialogue, and humble efforts to be open to the full truth are somehow thwarted.

One of the effects of the war-psychology which sprang up in these conflicts was to transform in retrospect the history of Marian doctrine into a series of victorious combats in which the champions of Mary had crushed their enemies. Conflicts and triumphs were thought up which bore little resemblance to the more peaceful and contemplative progress which was really that of dogmatic truth. A man who loved the Virgin Mary put himself in the place of a Cyril overcoming a Nestorius, a Scotus who had just defeated an army of learned doctors. By painting the past in such warlike colours, these myths laid the foundation for a future filled with strife. They produced a tendency to make further conquest seem preferable to peaceful possession of those truths which had already been acquired, "wordy battles" and dialectical argument to "the light of knowledge", in the words of St Augustine.[12]

Further, when polemic becomes by force of circumstances a necessity in the defence of what is essential, it acquires a degree of honour and respect, as killing men does in time of war. So Marian polemic has been elevated into a major act of devotion, and a virtue made of aggressiveness.

The heritage borne by the Marian movement is a heavy one.

Here again we must be careful not to be overdramatic. The dialectic, the workings of which we have just laid bare, went to nothing like its full extent. The power inherent in faith and charity to keep things on the right lines was not completely inoperative, as is proved by the attitude of a St Francis de Sales, a Camus or an Alphonsus Liguori and many others.[13] The controversial attitude may have caused damage to the tremendous activity of the seventeenth century but in its essentials it remained positive and constructive.

There are, however, two important, negative points to note: the immense output of work in the seventeenth century undoubtedly suffered as a result of not a little passionate impatience, and then, too, from its lack of knowledge of biblical or patristic sources. For example, the great wealth of good intentions and incredible efforts squandered in the quarrels over the *Avis salutaires*,[14] Maria de Agreda,[15] or the "vow of blood".[16] These produced results more unfortunate than fortunate.

To sum up briefly, it appears that the surprising phenomenon whose origins and distribution we have been trying to find, namely those tensions and conflicts within Catholicism of which the Virgin Mary is the object, is in fact very limited. Not only does it seem to be unknown in the East, and to pass unnoticed in large sections of the community in the West, but it is of very recent date. The Church possesses all the resources needed to overcome this particular crisis, but it will necessitate a clear and decisive effort.

The following causes for the appearance of the problem can be enumerated:

First of all, the growing pains of mariology in the Latin Church, above all the unilateral character of this growth since the fourteenth century. Growth has resulted far less from contemplation than from controversial reasoning and an analytical approach which has tended to isolate and dissociate the privileges of Mary from their true surroundings. It was in this way that the first Marian quarrels to which the title can properly be given arose round the doctrine of the Immaculate Conception.

Secondly we must place the indignation aroused by the adoption of an anti-Marian position by the Protestants, and the climate of bitter controversy which resulted from it.

Lastly, there is the confined and restricted outlook which is the other face of Marian specialization.

At this early stage we can already see several lessons which these conclusions can teach us. The specific remedies for the three factors mentioned above and the temporary crisis which has resulted from them would seem to include the consideration of a great deal of new basic material (notably from the East where no such conflicts have arisen), an ecumenical dialogue in the spirit of John XXIII, and a great widening of perspectives in such matters as the situating of the Virgin Mary in the Church, and the rethinking of Marian doctrine in its right place as part of the whole complex of dogma and Christian living.

These are the lessons we can learn from history.

III

The Two Tendencies Analysed

THE problems and the latent conflict which we attempted to
diagnose in the first chapter cannot be overcome merely by an
historical analysis. The lessons drawn from history can be very
enlightening, but they are not enough; we must try to understand what exactly these two opposing tendencies are—to give a
phenomenological analysis of them. Then we shall be able to look
for some means of resolving their antinomy.

1. THE SUPERFICIAL DUALITY AND THE ESSENTIAL UNITY

Before setting out on a path so beset with pitfalls of every kind,
it would be well to clear up two fundamental difficulties.

First of all, in taking the opinions of men as the object of
our study, we run the risk of being side-tracked from what is
really essential, from our real object, namely the dogma and the
deep life of the Church which continue unchanged beneath these
opinions, while on the surface men busy themselves opposing
one another. As we pursue our way, we must never forget the
essential unity. To do so would be a serious mistake.

The second preliminary difficulty, and my second scruple, is as
follows. These opinions and tendencies are generally reduced to
two, which are conceived of as being diametrically opposed. Is
this duality justified? Or is there not really here a much more
complex multiplicity? The variety of the facts would suggest this
view, which is reinforced by the discovery that scarcely anyone
will agree that he himself fits neatly into either of the two categories. Yet, whatever approach is followed, we always seem to
be led back to some kind of duality.

Our difficulty increases when we try to find names for the
tendencies, a thing which would greatly simplify our explanation of them. There is certainly an accepted terminology—
maximalists and *minimalists*—but these words have strange over-
tones for a theological issue. They suggest that we are dealing

with two parties and with a question of "more" or "less". The two terms have exactly the same sense and the same etymology as the Russian words which have now become international, Bolshevik and Menshevik—the party of the "more" and the party of the "less", the party of the possible maximum and that of compromise, the militants and the conciliatory. This philological comparison gives the whole question a political slant, and there is a real danger of our being led into asking if it is after all a question of right and left, of integrist and progressive, since the integrist is the conservative and therefore supposed to be on the right, and the progressive is the advanced man, on the left. Should we venture far in this direction, we shall come to some curious conclusions. Progressive thought in Marian matters often goes hand-in-hand with integrism in other areas, social and political as well as theological. Belief in progress in these matters usually goes with an integrist position in Marian affairs—a refusal to go ahead, coloured with a regret for the past, when the theology and the cultus of Mary had not developed to such an extent.[1]

Paradoxical as this may be, it at least shows us how relative these notions are. There is no progressive attitude which is not, in some respects at least, the complementary of an integrist one, and *vice versa*. Those who are partisans of daring evolution in the Church in social or liturgical affairs usually defend the *status quo*, or even the return to a less ardent past when it comes to questions of Marian and papal theology. Those who are all for the "*nunquam satis*"[2] and the "evolution of dogma" in what concerns our Lady and the teaching authority, generally advocate the *status quo* in other matters of dogma, for instance, or social affairs.

This is all very complex and confusing seen from outside, and yet it is written into the facts and immediately coherent to anyone who has grasped the dividing lines between the two points of view. A similar reversibility of attitudes can explain an analogous paradox in the political world, where those who foment liberating revolutions are often found to become dictators themselves if their revolution succeeds. If we are to try to get a complete insight into such problems we must first put our finger on the real root of the complexity. This means showing how the grouping into left and right is blurred by another: the grouping into extremists and moderates. It is this latter division which formally corresponds to that between the militants and the conciliatory, the prophets and the diplomats, the doctrinaire and the opportunists.

But considerations such as these are just the sort that can rouse tempers, and I have introduced them here only in order to banish them for good. Whether I like it or not, they cannot fail under one form or another to be at the back of the reader's mind, especially since they have made their appearance in the newspapers. Putting them in their correct place as relative and paradoxical is one way of casting them out. What we have to do is to get beyond this emotionally charged dialectic, and the illogical and constantly shifting attitudes of these disputes. We must deliver the Virgin Mary from the contamination with political or particularist notions into which men constantly try to drag her. A stop must be put to these quite unreal annexations by which one side tends to monopolize the Blessed Virgin so that she is correspondingly discredited on the other side.

Categories formulated with this idea of "more" or "less" in mind are therefore annoying in every respect. They force us to phrase the question at stake in terms of being more or less generous with Mary, or of increasing or diminishing her glory. Putting it in this way is to place it on a false plane of emotion, leaving theological criteria in the background. We should be starting from the most obvious results of the two attitudes, rather than from the explanation to be found for them in their origins. We should be entering on a path of ambiguity and misinterpretation from which we should never emerge.

Two alternative terms have been suggested recently : *christotypical* and *ecclesiotypical* mariology, one linking Mary to Christ, the other to the Church. Here we do find a more formal characteristic of the two tendencies, but there is nothing to show that this characteristic is in any way an essential one. More important, here again most people are very reluctant to let themselves be classified under either head, for in different degrees they are all trying to synthesize the two. This leads on to a vital consideration. We are in no way concerned with two blocs or two parties but with *two tendencies which are present together in the mind of every theologian*. It is the resultant combination which gives to each his particular outlook. We cannot insist too much on this point, for if it is not grasped the analysis which follows is going to be completely misunderstood. This analysis is a characterological one, and its objects will not be to catalogue two opposing categories of men but to determine the motive power behind the two tendencies, together with the attitudes and principal constituent parts which characterize them.

In one of my first articles which appeared in 1949,[3] I tried to characterize these two tendencies or attitudes, which, although opposed to each other, are never found in their pure state, by the use of the epithets *critical* and *mystical* or devotional. This terminology illustrates some of the characteristics of the two tendencies very well. One is very concerned with strict delineation, precise distinctions and an objective approach; the other is more personal and involved in life. The terminology answers very well to the state of the question in the seventeenth century, but it is much less adequate for the complexity of the present-day situation. In addition, such a terminology is not without ambiguity. It is essential to remember that we are dealing with a "critical" or a "devotional" attitude towards *the Blessed Virgin*, but that these epithets can easily be found interchanged in other domains. It would be completely erroneous to imagine that anyone who lacks a critical spirit must be a devotee of Mary, or that all those who have devotion to her are lacking the critical faculty. This terminology may be more pertinent and more fruitful, but it is still approximate and open to discussion, and it is still terribly irritating. We shall, therefore, try to avoid using such ambiguous labels without due consideration. But whatever may be the complexity of this duality, we are not going to be able to escape from the problem, for several authoritative papal documents, addressed precisely to mariologists, adopt dualist categories.

The radio message of Pius XII to the International Congress of 1954 might be mentioned, together with the *motu proprio* of John XXIII making the Mariological Academy in Rome into a Pontifical Academy. They insist that mariology, built on sound, solid doctrine, should be on its guard "on the one hand, against any falsifying and excessive exaltation that goes beyond what truth allows, and, on the other hand, against an excessive timidity limiting the dignity of the Mother of God".[4] In these documents the pontiffs would have us beware of the circumstances which lead to errors either through excess or through deficiency. The solution of the problem must, therefore, be sought along these lines.

In our examination, we shall approach the question first from the point of view of the possible theological opinions, and then from that of devotion to Mary.

2. THE THEOLOGICAL ASPECT

At Marian congresses the division between the two tendencies of opinion becomes obvious when it comes to the drafting of the resolutions. Those of one outlook are inclined to want many of these, the others none at all, or very few The few of which they would approve would not be directed to the same end as those of the others. Here the question is indeed one of "more" or "less", but it is also one of orientation.

Let us start with the easiest of the two, this idea of "more" and "less". The first are for increasing the number of Marian dogmas. After fighting for and winning the definition of the Assumption they now look for new "conquests" (to follow the terminology in use in the most committed Marian *milieux*). Often they go so far as to propose a long programme of definitions—the mediation, the co-redemption, the queenship, the spiritual motherhood and so on.

The others are for the *status quo*. In their opinion, to make an increase in the number of Marian dogmas an end in itself is a preoccupation foreign to the main stream of theology; it is a truly Marian speciality! They see in it a complete reversal of priorities and values, implying the use of infallibility as a servant of devotion, or even as an instrument for some public-relations undertaking.

There is the same disagreement about liturgical feasts.

Since the seventeenth century, the most fervent clients of the Virgin Mary have never stopped agitating for new feasts, in spite of the coolness shown by the Congregation of Rites. The others would agitate, on the contrary, for the cleaning-up of the liturgy by removing the large number of modern innovations which overload and disfigure it. These additions remind them of Viollet-le-Duc's buttresses added to Notre-Dame, or of the sham ornaments with which some Romanesque churches have been encumbered in recent centuries.

A quantitative *more* or *less* such as we see here (more or less feasts or dogmas) is found again in the general picture of doctrinal

57

positions. Some tend to interpret dogmas and doctrines in the maximum sense, the others in the minimum sense. (This is where the expressions "maximalists" and "minimalists" find their most accurate application.)

To take the Immaculate Conception as an example, some eliminate all "debt of sin", to such an extent that it becomes practically impossible to see exactly from what and in respect of what the Virgin Mary needed to be redeemed. The others tend to give weight and substance to the heritage of sin which weighed upon Mary as a daughter of Adam, or even to reify it. They would go so far as to maintain the presence in her of what medieval theologians called the *infectio carnis* (the disposition to sin transmitted through the flesh), and even of concupiscence, or an inclination to evil.[5]

As far as the fullness of grace linked to the Immaculate Conception is concerned, some insist on seeing this privilege in the light of the glories of Mary, others emphasize its fundamental gratuity. The former, following the lead of the *Mariale* (supposedly of Albertus Magnus), sometimes delight in detailing the content and the prerogatives of this fullness, of which the first would be (they maintain) a conscious supernatural life for Mary from the first instant of her existence.

In the matter of the divine motherhood, the dogma as it was affirmed at the Council of Ephesus eliminates all possibility of error on the side of deficiency. The substance of this dogma is so profound that over- or underestimations, wide or narrow explanations, all seem like specks of dust compared with the greatness of the essential core. Nevertheless, some insist on the *necessity* of the links between this motherhood and Mary's sanctity; the others see the connection as a *free decision* of the divine will. Some insist almost exclusively on the function of this motherhood—as the means and the instrument of the incarnation; others on the greatness of the privilege and the glory implied in it for the Theotokos. They put Mary's belonging to the hypostatic order in the foreground, as we have seen, and wish to attribute to her an instrumental efficient causality in this union. Sometimes they go so far as to make this thesis the necessary condition for the safeguard of the dogma of the divine motherhood. They feel that without it the dogma would be reduced to a mere verbal affirmation. In general one opinion prefers to think in terms of the downward ("Cyrillian") movement which puts the immediate personal relationship of Mary with the Incarnate Word in the foreground, her act in giving birth being seen as the means whereby this supreme relationship is brought about; the other opinion prefers the upward movement which starts from Mary's maternal functions and ascends to the divinity of the Son whom she bears according to the flesh.

Concerning the virginity of Mary, one opinion interprets Luke I. 34 as a vow made by Mary prior to the Annunciation, the other rejects this interpretation. For the representatives of this opinion it was through the angel's message that the intention to keep her virginity arose in her. The ideas of the virginity before and after the delivery provoke little debate, but that of virginity in the actual act of giving birth is the source of great disagreement. One point of view goes so far as to interpret the virginity *in partu* as meaning nothing short of a delivery *utero clauso* in which Mary played no active part; the other goes to the other extreme, even questioning the facts, which have been accepted without discussion for fifteen centuries, that Mary kept virginal integrity in her body as well as in her soul and that she gave birth without pain.

The definition of the dogma has cut short discussion of the basic point of the Assumption, the actual bodily presence of Mary with the Risen Christ. But some tend to reduce to a minimum any idea of privilege that may be expressed in the Assumption : it is after all nothing more than a temporal priority. Some, holding an extreme view, think that, since eternity has no relationship with time and since the soul is the formal reason for the individuation of the body, the resurrection coincides for every man with his entry into glory. (Such theses are only hinted at, but it is a fact that they are current.) Others, on the contrary, insist upon the unique privilege of this Assumption. Similarly, some see Mary's death as an ordinary death from illness or old age, just like that which overtakes any human organism; others speak of a "death of love", or make of it a kind of undimensional instant, some kind of nominal death; yet others think that Mary did not die, but was simply taken (*assumpta*) body and soul into heaven at the glorious end of her terrestrial destiny.

On the subject of the queenship, one opinion gives Mary the prerogatives of a queen with effective powers of government;

others those of a queen-mother, linked very intimately with her son who alone governs, after the fashion suggested by the traditional biblical figure of Bathsheba (3 Kings 2. 19; cf. 3. 31). Here we can see again the disagreement between those who give Mary the function of a head in the mystical body, and those who prefer to see her as its heart.

With the Redemption, there is no dogmatic definition to restrain the freedom of opinions, and the two extreme positions taken up are the following. In the first, Mary's co-operation is limited to her role in the incarnation of Christ and in the diffusion or application of grace. The second sees her as having in addition brought about the Redemption itself in such a way that her merit was sufficient to obtain it in justice, even though it is in fact subordinated to the superabundant merit of Christ.

One opinion puts her mediation in the front line, the other finds it troublesome. The first gives a definite shape to the pattern which makes the Virgin Mary an intermediary set up between Christ and ourselves, to pass on for us what we send to him and back to us in return the graces given by Christ. Mary is made into an instrumental cause in the strict sense and into a universal instrumental cause. The other view tends to reduce the part of Mary purely and simply to one of intercession.

The two patterns would materially be as follows:

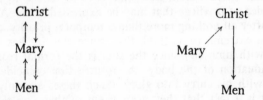

The first reproaches the other with separating us from Mary, since, there, Christ alone seems to be in direct contact with men. The second reproaches the first with separating us from Christ, since there it is Mary alone who seems to be in contact with us.

As we conclude this bird's-eye view in which the situation has been reduced to a few broad lines, it is important for us to avoid an oversimplified and false interpretation according to which we should have on the one hand the maximalists who would defend all the maximalist theories we have listed, and the minimalists on the other adopting systematically all the minimalist syntheses. It is in fact only a matter of the dominating influence in a particular outlook. For example, on the question of our Lady's death, the Spanish theologians who are normally supposed to illustrate the outlook which is most attracted to the theses which are "generous towards Mary" are strongly opposed to the idea of her being immortal, for they have a very strong national tradition about her death. The key to these divergencies does not lie, therefore, in any question of "more" or "less". I have heard the problem treated at certain discussions between mariologists in a very superficial fashion. At these I have heard someone asked why, as a minimalist, he held a certain maximalist theory, or *vice versa*. Such a dialectical approach has no meaning for a theologian who tries to judge solely on theological criteria. The tendency to "more" or to "less" plays only an infinitely small part in exerting a remote influence on certain opinions.

The important thing is to find out the fundamental inspirations of the two tendencies.

One is dominated by love. This has its advantages and its disadvantages. Its advantage is that love gives a connaturality which is an aid to the deepening of one's knowledge of the other. Its disadvantage is the ever-present risk of projecting on to the object the emotional desires of the subject. The other tendency is dominated by a concern not to falsify the true facts by introducing into them such reasons from the heart as true Reason knows nothing of. Nothing is more difficult than to decide the ideal place for the dividing line. Fundamentally the first point of view would seem to have the advantage, for theology cannot be alien to love since God is love and saves us by inviting us to love him. But this love must remain clear-sighted and free from any superfluous or falsifying infatuations. It can be nourished by nothing but the truth.

On another plane, another contrast. This is a correlative of the first and is that between *seeing* and *doing*. On one side there is a practical attitude dominated by a concern to glorify Mary and add new jewels to her crown. On the other is a speculative approach with no other concern than the perception of revealed truth : Marian theology is for them a matter of scrupulous precision and factual investigation, rather than of building a structure with the aim of glorifying Mary. Here we must agree with the *second* point of view, for theology is essentially a speculative science as completely subject to facts as to the object of faith. If it is in one sense tied to a *praxis*—that of charity—it is so simply in its method of action. It is not *doing* in the way in which an art that creates its object is *doing*. Some might point to the words of Christ in St John's Gospel (3. 21): "He who *does the truth* comes to light." In fact this really means: "He who conforms his conduct to divine truth . . .", and Mollat is right in interpreting it as: "He who *acts in the truth* . . .". Such an activity may include in its scope works of charity, but it certainly does not refer to the activities of a theologian whose aim is to construct new truths. The true attitude of the theologian is pre-eminently contemplative.

This is why, after agreeing with the attitude linked with charity, which has its part to play in Marian as in any other theology, we must go on to agree with a speculative in preference to a constructive approach.

In the orientations which give rise to their methods of approaching the subject the following differences are revealed by the two tendencies.

The one is interested above all in the person of Mary, the other in her function within the whole picture of the mystery of salvation.

The first is, therefore, led to accentuate the immanence of God's gift, the other the transcendence of the God who gives. The first accentuates the merits of Mary (following from this the attempt is sometimes made to find grounds for saying that she merited for herself her first grace, or at least that she merited *de condigno* both her divine maternity and the redemption); the second accentuates the free gift of the divine generosity at the very beginning of her destiny, at the great moment of her life when she was made the Mother of God, and, indeed, at other times.

So the one tendency is, to insist on the logicality, the coherence and, in fact, the unity of her destiny, on the necessary inter-connection of her privileges; the other, to insist on the twofold liberty of God and Mary who together bring this destiny into effect. The first tendency, therefore, is to think in terms of *theologia,* that is to say, of a speculative deepening of knowledge of the object (here that ontological structure of which the divine maternity is generally considered the fundamental *ratio* and measure). The other is to think in terms of *oeconomia,* which is just another way of saying salvation history. The role of Mary is considered as a function of that history into which she had the mission of introducing Christ.

In the first, emphasis is laid on the glories of Mary, in the other, on her poverty, her humility, her status as a servant; the first thinks of her transcendence over the Church, the other of her membership of the community of the redeemed; from one side the Church in Mary, from the other Mary in the Church.

In a word, the first mode of thought seeks to establish an organic unity in the person of Mary, the other in the great events of the scheme of salvation. Two different outlooks on predestination are implied here. In the one, everything is willed for Mary the Queen in the unity of Christ the King; in the other, Mary is willed in her place in the whole scheme of salvation in which Christ came down from heaven "for us men and for our salvation— *propter nos homines et propter nostram salutem"*, as we say in the Creed.

Here we have probably come to the deepest difference between the two emphases. For one side, the supremacy of Mary compared to all other creatures is foremost, together with the staggering feat of her participation in the divinity of her Son. For the others, the important thing is the transcendence of Christ and the incommensurable primacy of his divinity which must not at any price be obscured or minimized. To do this would be in their opinion the gravest possible form of minimalism.

So the first try to bring into prominence all that there is in common between Christ and Mary, using the same expressions of each if it is possible : Christ is God, but Mary also is divine, and strictly so, not in her womanhood but in her motherhood. She belongs as does Christ to the hypostatic order of which she alone among the redeemed is a member. She is the only one who like him was immaculate in her conception, full of grace and not liable to sin. He is the Redeemer, she is the redemptrix. He is the Mediator, she is the mediatrix. She alone has been glorified in her body like him. There are certain mariologists who like to apply systematically to Mary the great christological texts and even liturgical prayers addressed to God. (Thus in the Middle

Ages a *Te Mariam Laudamus* was composed parallel in every way to the *Te Deum Laudamus*.)

The others put first the things that are shared in common by Mary and the other members of Christ. Like all Christians, Mary was truly and properly redeemed, although in a more perfect and a higher way. The grace she has is of the same kind as that which others have and differs from it only in degree. Like her, we are gratuitously set free from original sin; the only difference is that she was preserved from it while we are delivered from it. Her resurrection does not differ from ours except by temporal anticipation. If she co-operates in the Redemption, so do all other Christians, "fellow workers for God", as St Paul calls them (1 Cor. 3. 9). If she is a mediatrix, we too are mediators in the One, the Only Mediator. She is Queen, but we also reign with Christ. Finally, on the subject of the divine motherhood, they insist on the *concepit prius mente quam corpore*[6] current among the Fathers of the Church. If it was Mary alone who bore Christ, it is given to each of us to "conceive him in our hearts by faith".

In short, in one point of view the basic division in the scheme of things is situated between the ontological transcendence of God and the humble status of the creature; in the other, it comes between the spotless holiness which is found only in Christ and Mary and the status of those who are involved in sin. In a sense it is a question of perspective. To the ancients the moon appeared to be one inaccessible star among all the others. From a nebula it would appear as a satellite quite close to the earth, almost as much a part of it as the rings are of Saturn. So, depending on the perspective chosen, Mary will be placed among the redeemed set against Christ, or at the side of Christ set against the sinners who pray to her.

In their extreme forms, one outlook will turn the treatise on Mary into a carbon copy of the treatise on Christ, and for those who think along these lines, the fundamental principle of mariology is the perfect association and assimilation of Mary with her Son. The other outlook would make the treatise a copy of that on the Church (looked at, needless to say, from its mystical aspect and excluding the external and hierarchical aspect), and those who hold this view will show how Mary is in every way the first, the exemplary realization of the gifts which are bestowed in the Church: she is the *type of the Church*.

Some have seen in this the fundamental principle of Marian theology.

3. MARIAN DEVOTION

The same tendencies, accompanied by certain distinctive nuances and outward manifestations, appear when we examine Marian devotion.

On one side, the most advanced and most dogmatic doctrinal positions will be expressed in striking devotional formulae, while those of the other outlook will be irritated and incited by these to a negative attitude of denial and disaffection. Such words as unbalanced, excessive, will come to their lips, while the others will in turn consider them lukewarm and lacking in understanding.

Here once again the inclination towards two distinct categories of themes and two ways of approaching them appears. On one side, we shall be presented with the glory and the power of Mary; on the other, with her humility and her faith. Those of one opinion will show a servile devotion to Mary as Queen; those of the other will prefer the imitation of Mary, the handmaid of the Lord. On one side, her mediation will be emphasized with great insistence upon the way this takes place and the images which are used to illustrate it—the canal, the aqueduct, the "neck of the Church", and so on. The other side will be intensely irritated by such formulations, finding them distasteful because they introduce something between Christ and the Christian, and far worse, because they obscure the immediate character of his presence in our souls which is the very foundation of grace.

The attitude taken towards apparitions is another component of the problem which is prominent when we are examining it on the plane of devotion. From one side they will be given the maximum possible significance. In the most extreme cases they can become the whole of religion; a sect of this or that apparition springs up with its view limited by its self-imposed blinkers. From the other side this is answered by a certain coolness and, indeed, a distrust of all apparitions. It will be frequently pointed out that the facts concerning such exceptional acts of the supernatural do not bind dogmatically. We shall be reminded that it is possible to be saved without believing in either Lourdes or Fatima, since the reality of neither apparition is an article of faith. Certainly theologians who hold the first point of view have recently challenged the classical opinion, until now never questioned, which left the conscience completely free in this matter. According to this new opinion, the Church's authority can now be said to impose belief in the reality of the apparition at Lourdes as a matter of dogmatic fact.

This is a significant difference, for it means that we could use the various gradations of opinion about the various apparitions as a standard of measuring the degree of commitment of a person to one point of view or the other. On the side of reserve, many would accept Lourdes after a certain effort, La Salette would be more difficult, Fatima much more difficult still. On the Marian side, on the contrary, it is Fatima which inspires the most passionate commitment. The strange newspaper article in which the bishops were accused in the name of a Catholicism which was all but reduced to this single apparition has already been mentioned.

On the level of piety, then, once again a tendency towards abundance on one side (the multiplication of Marian prayers and activities), and, on the other, an inclination to sparseness and abstention make their appearance.

On this level the most significant constituent elements are the following:

First of all, among those of one view Marian devotion tends to hold the central position. It is supreme and in extreme cases holds the field alone. Among those of the other outlook it is discreet, it is correctly integrated and unobtrusive, and in the extreme it may be completely absent. Those who see things in this way will be very conscious of the undesirable elements, the excesses and the deviations in Marian piety. Down these two slippery paths we can fall into either a "Marian" Christianity which St Paul would certainly not recognize as such or a Christianity without Mary which would no longer be Catholic.

The fact is that one side tends to exalt Marian devotion into a panacea. Love the Virgin, develop a deep devotion to her and anything else that is needed in personal life as well as for the apostolate and for the good of the Church will be supplied as well. Practise Marian devotion and you will by that very act attain to sanctity, to supernatural efficacy, to salvation. Get a new dogma defined, consecrate the world to Mary, introduce a new form of devotion and the present perils of the Church will vanish. Such themes recur frequently in the writings of Marian mystics from the end of the Middle Ages onwards, and particularly since the seventeenth century.

For those holding the other opinion, what matters is the message of salvation proclaimed by Christ in the Gospel. That is what is essential and it is sufficient. Mary certainly has her place in this message, but she does not appear as the basic and fundamental element in it. They show no enthusiasm for, and object to, the things which are advocated by those of the other outlook. The tacit or explicit axioms of a certain kind of Marian piety seem to them to obscure what is essential and to give rise to facile thinking, and lead to illusions. It suggests the substitution of quasi-magical little tricks for the deep demands of the Sermon on the Mount. For them the important thing is to set Marian devotion in its right place and orientate it in such a way as to encourage the Christian message to flourish in its completeness, namely in the gift of the whole self to God and in the apostolate.

For this reason such quick recipes for salvation are seen by them to be an illusion since they cause the real problem to be forgotten and deaden the impact of the demands of such commitments as are adapted to the world of reality.

Consecrations to Mary present them with further difficulties. On this subject their queries are many. The possibility of consecration to anyone except God is one, with a question whether the consecration made in baptism is not sufficient. They question the need to add any more and feel that the desire arises in others because this fundamental consecration has been forgotten. The large-scale, collective consecrations made by limited groups astonish them even more, especially when in them are included non-believers. What sense is there is such consecrations since they are not sacraments, having an *ex opere operato* value, but sacramentals whose worth resides in the *opus operantis*, the free self-committal in faith of those who are consecrating themselves?[7] All of this strikes them as far removed from the theology of St Thomas, and as coming dangerously close to magical ideas about the supernatural.

As to this idea that new definitions or the promotion of new doctrinal developments in Marian matters would be a remedy for the perils threatening the Church, they are of opinion that neither theology nor—seeing that so many such measures were taken in the last century—experience justifies such maxims. Not only did the definition of the Immaculate Conception not arrest the development of materialism, it created a division between Catholics and Eastern Christians as well as Protestants.

The holders of the first point of view would answer these objections by saying that they show a too materialistic view of things. Even if the new Marian definitions do seem to have given rise to new ecumenical difficulties, they must also have borne some fruit in that cause, however unseen and lying beneath the surface. The proclamation of the truth is in all circumstances supremely timely, and the apparent opposition of conflicting timely actions is an illusion borne of a too materialistic view of history. They are shocked that anyone should seriously question this view.

In regard to this first constituent element, it is certain that the Blessed Virgin is not the one absolutely essential thing, yet, at the same time, she is closely linked to it. She can have a dominant place in certain phases of life for certain individuals and groups of people as a result of events, of a personal decision or a particular grace. Marian devotion can act as an inspiration, giving direction to all the rest of the devotional life and moulding its development along the right lines. Here there is need for a very alert pastoral sense in regard to both individuals and circumstances, for diversity is inherent in the devotional life. It is no domain for rigidity and abstractions. The temptation to set oneself up as a judge over others without taking sufficient note of their particular situation is to be guarded against, especially when one has no authority to do so. It would be even worse to set up one's own approach as the universal norm. Above all one must guard against irritation and bitterness, for these are contrary to charity as well as to all sound devotion to Mary. On the other hand, Marian devotion cannot be made into a panacea, nor into a norm to measure all other forms of devotion. It must be "well ordered", which means properly situated in the whole complex of devotion. Beyond the objective norms of conformity to the Church in letter and in spirit, one of the greatest criteria for evaluating it remains the advice in the Gospel: "The tree is known by its fruits" (Matt. 12. 33; cf. 7. 16-19).

A second constituent going to make up the picture is seen in the way one attitude gives shape to Marian devotion by means of devotional formulae, societies, activities and practices which it delights in multiplying, while, by the other, it is kept down to only the most binding obligations.

In the one there is the danger of overabundance and above all of materialization; in the other, Marian piety can easily be reduced to its simplest possible mode of expression, if not lost altogether through disuse.

By force of circumstance the first kind of excess will retain our main attention, not because it is necessarily the most frequent or the most dangerous, but because, as distinct from the other (emptiness needs but few words to describe it), it presents all kinds of different variations. Without going into too many details, for these are not well defined anyway, enough must be said to enable us to draw one or two essential conclusions.

It is a matter of fact that from the end of the Middle Ages until at least the eighteenth century Marian piety produced more and more "prescriptions for salvation" tied up with tangible, material, quantitative means. Heaven or some other benefit was assured by the wearing of a medal or the recitation of a particular formula. Here we can discern a tendency to narrow down devotion, to materialize it, and, by so doing, to corrupt it. The Church has discreetly restrained abuses in this sphere. Nevertheless, although this materializing tendency has lost ground, it is certainly not dead. Only in recent years a campaign was launched to get 100,000 or more Masses said to obtain the definition of the mediation. Can it be said that the pursuit of such aims really shows a balanced appreciation of the respective functions of the faith of the people, the Church's teaching authority, and the sacrifice of the death of Christ? Rather this mathematical approach would lead us to imagine that the number of Masses said has more value in the eyes of God than the faith and charity with which priest and people take part in the sacrifice. It tends to make us forget that the multiplication of celebrations has no other function than to make present, in time and in every place where men live, the unique redeeming sacrifice. In short, such undertakings, however well intentioned they may be, surely run counter to the demands of a religion "in spirit and in truth".

At the very bottom of this particular slope we come across definite superstitions. These do exist, and Grignion de Montfort was not ignorant of the fact. He strongly criticized a purely "external" Marian devotion which is satisfied with such materialism in its practices, and a "presumptuous" devotion which, under the pretext of piety, becomes ever more deeply involved in sin. The true love of the Virgin Mary which was his ran out of words with which to stigmatize sufficiently this hypocritical attitude covering, as it does, sin "under the mantle of the faithful Virgin". In this connection his tone seems to equal Luther's violence: "Nothing in our Christian religion is so worthy of condemnation as this diabolical presumption . . . it is a most horrible sacrilege . . . and, next to the sacrilege of an unworthy Communion, the greatest and the least pardonable."[8]

It is the poverty of a certain kind of Marian devotion which lies at the root of these abuses. For the want of true enlightenment zeal is diverted into mediocre and facile ways which lead on into far worse corruptions.

Another source of this disfigurement is the way in which the superstition that still lingers in men's hearts seeks to find its satisfaction in the Church itself the moment the rectifying power of faith ceases to keep things in order. A good woman who goes about the markets selling medals, worried by her customers' lack of Christian instruction, recently wrote to me and said: "It is good-luck charms, not faith they are looking for. This is something that has become increasingly the case in the last three or four years. . . . I was working one day at P— alongside a fortune-teller who was selling lucky mascots. He had a great crowd round him. I had to leave for I had no customers. My predecessor told me: 'You never sell anything next to them. People have more confidence in those talismans than in a holy medal'" (letter dated 25 March, 1963).

Such facts as the above set a problem which we must not be too ready to consider solved. How do we distinguish between the flax which is still smouldering and the flax which is out, between the action which helps to restore a person to the Church and the action that gives a too easy reassurance to religious anxieties, but in so doing stops all chance of real conversion and turns into wrong channels the hidden force which was perhaps leading towards it? How do we distinguish between the wearing of a medal from a Christian motive and that by which the image of the Blessed Virgin is lowered to the level of a purely magical lucky charm?

Whatever theory we may put forward, we should do well to remember the words of Grignion de Montfort concerning those whose devotion springs from selfish motives only, "who have recourse to our Lady only to win some lawsuit, to escape some danger, to be cured of some illness or for some similar need. . . . All these are false followers and are acceptable neither to God nor to his holy Mother."[9]

A third element is found in the difference between the great emotional fervour generated by Marian devotion on the one hand, and the great coldness shown towards it on the other. The former may lead to the evils of excess and wrong-headedness, the latter to those of disaffection and indifference.

This pair of distinctions bring us up against the great problem of the place of emotion in Marian piety. This subject is so delicate that it can only possibly be considered fruitfully in the light of a very deep faith. It is really the problem of the place of emotional involvement in the Christian life as a whole. Its role is a secondary one, as an accessory, but it must not be underestimated. If faith is essentially a spiritual act of the will and of the intelligence, it does nevertheless involve the whole man and must therefore affect the feelings and the emotions. By faith these are caught up, purified, refashioned and put right. We have only to look back to the writings of the prophets, the Gospels and the works of the most detached of Christian mystics like St John of the Cross to grasp the place of the heart and the affections which go with it. Christ surely had a human affection for his Father. And has this not come down to us through the apostles and across the Christian centuries? It goes without saying that emotional engagement has not the same stability and permanence as faith. It comes and goes. It can be completely cut off without harm, and normally such an experience would be a good rather than a bad thing. Furthermore, the affections have their own inclinations, their own appetites. They are by nature greedy, excessive, insatiable, prone to go astray, in the supernatural order no less than in the natural order. Whence the necessity of keeping them subordinated to the light of faith and, by it, of correcting them. We must not be astonished. The purest affective themes in the Gospel can be just as easily corrupted by the errors of the human emotions as any other. Thus certain minds can falsify and distort even the profound revelation Christ made of his Father who is also "our Father", making it the forbidding picture of a father *à la Kafka*, or, just the opposite, turning him into a kindly old man, an indulgent old sugar-daddy grandfather. To overcome such deviations is, therefore, an important task for the sake of the internal equilibrium as well as the outward witness of Christianity. Our psychology-minded age makes us see what a delicate task this is, and what a degree of tact and fineness of touch it demands. It is made all the more necessary by the fact that Marian devotion, when it seems to be losing momentum, is sometimes tempted to seek renewed vigour in exploiting false images that are designed to arouse the emotions.

In connection with Marian piety the affections can enter the picture in two ways, depending on whether Mary is seen as a woman or as a mother.

I have sometimes heard it said (frequently by people whose devotion to Mary was of a high standard) that the sublimation of the need for a woman's presence was an important element in Marian devotion. After long years of thought I have come to the conclusion that this view is exaggerated and inaccurate. One sweeping observation must suffice. Marian devotion is neither more prevalent nor more intense among men than among women. In fact the great bulk of fervent devotion is found among women. Yet we must not dismiss this factor as completely non-existent. It has at times in past centuries given rise to forms of devotion which are really surprising, and which were fruitful in images and in rites, and, I was going to say, using the word in its modern sense, in characteristic myths. The most typical is the practice of a mystical marriage with Mary which is to be found in the works of a whole line of spiritual writers beginning with Alain de la Roche (d. 1475). In the most ardent cases this gave rise to a complete ritual with the wearing of a ring to signify the marriage, and sometimes even a map of Loveland describing all the stages in the consummation of the union. But such extreme forms are rare exceptions. They can perhaps be excused by admitting that the emotional language of love has always been used in Christian spirituality, after the model of the *Song of Songs*, and that such language expresses a purer and more spiritual reality than at first would appear. Yet this analogy has little value here, for the latter deals with the spiritual relationship between the soul and the transcendent God. The same language and the same images are more dangerous when they concern a human being like our Lady. But at least we can take into consideration and admit certain attenuating circumstances. First of all, we are dealing with individual cases of people who had no intention of founding a school of thought. Then, seen from inside, these seem to have been attempts to overcome cases of serious lack of balance. Viewed in this way, they are seen as doing more to sublimate and rectify these tendencies than would appear from quoting this or that isolated text. We can distinguish from these extreme cases certain spiritual writers of the French School who have refined the idea. The idea of a "marriage" is reduced by them to one of a "union" and such traces as may remain of a too materialistic symbolism are very slight. The current development of psychoanalysis has made contemporary thought allergic to this type of devotion in any case, and there is, therefore, no point in wasting more time over it.

There is no need either for us to stop to examine the suggestion that "courtly love" provided the origin for mediaeval devotion to Mary. It may be admitted that there were some projections of this way of thought into it, but the importance of such occurrences as there were has been unjustifiably magnified. It was certainly no more than a very secondary and superficial factor. A systematic study of the relevant texts proves this beyond argument.

No more weight need be given to another theory which appears from time to time : the theory suggesting that mariology is built on the myth of the "eternal feminine", in the finest sense of the word. However purified and rightly adjusted that theme may be, it can still give rise on frequent occasions to metaphorico-metaphysical extravaganzas which completely swallow up the Virgin of the Gospels. Sometimes the legend branches off into the question of "androgyny". It certainly tends to turn the Virgin Mary into an abstract and impersonal hypostasis offensive both to the theology of the humble mother of the Lord, and to the theology of the Holy Ghost. But again, this is of only secondary importance and need not detain us longer

Much more important is the second kind of emotional approach, the one that comes to Mary as mother. When Tradition is examined, the astonishing fact emerges that this is of relatively recent emergence, for the rare and vague hints which appear in the Patristic period cannot be taken as representative. Christians only came to consider Mary formally as *their* mother in the ninth or tenth century and, above all, in the eleventh and twelfth. St Bernard knows nothing of this sentiment; for him Mary is his queen, not his mother.[10] In the East the idea is also of late development and remains exceptional, the cultus of Mary as Mother *of God* there overshadows everything else.[11] Thus the great number of the themes, practices and rites which we must now look at date from relatively recent times and come only from the West.

Even if the theological bases for this filial attitude can be held to be firm and indisputable, grounded as they are on the words of Christ: "Behold thy mother" (John 19. 26-7), the question arises as to the degree to which the filial feeling should be taken, together with the orientation and coloration it should have, remembering that it is one of the strongest and most deeply rooted instincts in the heart of man.

On the surface it appears supremely simple and pure, yet depth psychology (leaving aside the more exaggerated forms of this) has shown it to be one of the most complex and confused feelings man has. Great numbers of men spend their whole lives fighting their "maternal complex" without ever escaping from it. The most widely accepted school of psychology tells us of deviations in the maternal instinct, the most frequent being the possessive form (Mauriac's *Genitrix*), which brings infantilism in its train as its counterpart in the person to whom it is directed. We cannot escape from the impression that certain abuses in Marian devotion spring from the attempt to find emotional satisfaction for an infantile tendency which feels the need of refuge and security, or that they project on to Mary the character and disposition of a possessive mother who demands, by a kind of emotional blackmail, a closed and undivided love. Marian piety must be on guard against such a disgraceful thing, for this is not the Mother of God, our heavenly Mother, who is concerned about our union with Christ and the development of our adult and mature outlook. Just as care must be taken to treat with mistrust the intrusion of certain femininity myths into Marian piety, so also it must be exercised against certain maternity myths. Even though they are found in the works of reputable authors, we would do well to use great discernment in welcoming such themes as that of a return to the maternal womb of Mary, of a "gestation" in her which, it is suggested, is our state until we are born into heaven. Such an image corresponds to a repressive tendency, a refusal of life and its responsibilities which is essentially unhealthy. I grant that it can have a right use, but it could not be taught today without giving occasion for scandal and for disaffection for Marian devotion. I say this with some particular cases in mind.

The value of the fundamental theme of motherhood and the spiritual health which springs from it should not be misconceived because of the critical analysis of these dangers which has been made here. This is too evident to need insisting on, as both history and pastoral experience bear witness. I should just like to remark that the equilibrium and sane motivation of this filial affection will be strengthened if the close link between Mary's motherhood and that of the Church is grasped. It is a spiritual motherhood within the mystery of Christ, a humble motherhood in the Holy Spirit who transcends and makes us to pass beyond the narrow confines of our human psychology.

There is one last myth which has been like a dangerous gangrene in a whole stream of Marian devotion. This has set masculine brutality against the unfailing tenderness of the mother who protects her children against the anger of the male. It is almost incredible that such a myth could have been shamelessly applied to Christ and Mary. And yet it is a fact that there is a school of iconography (which has now disappeared) in which Jesus is depicted armed with a bow or a thunderbolt which he brandishes in anger against sinners, while Mary intercedes for them, baring her maternal breast to move him to pity. It is just as alarming to find that a seventeenth-century author with an otherwise good reputation should have let himself go so far as to write: "Jesus wishes to condemn, Mary to save."[12] Whatever the good intentions, such a statement is objectively blasphemous. The mercy of Mary is nothing but a sharing in the mercy of God. She herself comes from God's mercy. She is a particularly sensitive sign of it that he himself has made for us. Mary's intercession makes no sense except when seen in this light.

One good thing about the psychological discoveries of the present century is that they provide the wherewithal for a purification of Marian piety. This cleansing should put right and strengthen; it should not be destructive. For the expression of filial feeling in a personal and inventive way is not something to be got rid of, it is quite normal. It must, however, be discreet and modest; what Mauriac called "the scandal of the strong" must not be forgotten. To quote a simple example: I have known circles of fervent devotees in France in which they love using the pet word "*Maman*" instead of "Mother" because it gave greater satisfaction to a need for tenderness and intimacy. I have even known some where the word was introduced in place of *Mary* in the *Hail Mary*. It was done with much fineness of feeling, to be sure, but I happened to find out that even in these circles themselves this modification of the Church's form of words was felt by some to be a burden and a hindrance.

This outline of the dangers which can threaten Marian piety in its affective activity and genius must not make us forget the fundamental fact. Devotion to Mary is usually a balancing factor in the right ordering of the emotions. By it men can peacefully get beyond many of the troubles of human emotional life, so often unbalanced through egoism and excess. Once this has been accomplished, it can give Christian affection a disinterestedness, a detachment, a discretion, a purity, a refinement, a self-forgetfulness, a sense of authentic silence, and in the end an evangelical transparency which are, after all, not so very rare, and which are graces coming from the mystery of Nazareth, graces it pleases Christ to give to the poor in spirit who are, in a special way, in contact with the "low estate of his handmaiden" (Luke 1. 48).

4. DISCRIMINATION

We can see from these examples how each of the two tendencies, the manifestations of which we have just examined, can commend itself in valuable ways, but each, at the same time, implies its own danger. Neither, therefore, can be canonized as it stands; neither the one nor the other can claim our undivided allegiance as it stands.

The "Marian" tendency is right when it looks at the Blessed Virgin without misgivings, holding in high honour the unique function and dignity which are hers in the history of salvation and in Christian theology. It is right to make its own the filial yearning of the Church towards Mary, the Mother of God, who is the high point of its communion with Christ. But in its flight, this tendency always carries the risk of going beyond its aim, or of turning aside, rather like a quick and impatient horse which drags the whole team of horses and the plough to one side and so spoils the straight line of the furrow.

There are several points at which we find these deviations at work.

First there is the danger of forgetting, eclipsing or relegating the primacy of Christ either by confusing Mary's functions and privileges with his through not using sufficiently differentiated terms to describe them, or, even, by seeing some sort of deficiency in the human Christ which it is Mary's mission to make good. Thus according to certain theories which have, it must be added, had little success, since Christ was not a human person, the consent of Mary, who was no more than a creature, was necessary to ratify the redemption in the name of humanity. According to others, she is for this same reason closer to us and more merciful than Christ himself. Here monophysite tendencies can be seen, and the decisions of the Councils that Christ is perfect Man and perfect Redeemer must be recalled against these.

There is a further danger that the Marian aspect of Christian devotion will be artificially and systematically magnified. Excess or, rather, quantitative disproportion, verbal or conceptual extravagance, sentimental overstatement and excrescences in the form of myths may all appear. The Church has always been careful to avoid such excesses. Her discreet and effective role in doing this has never been the subject of study as such, yet it is an aspect of the exercise of her teaching authority which is both edifying and instructive.

I shall not return to the dangers inherent in any attempt at over-precision or excessive specialization; they were adequately examined in the first chapter.

It is enough to insist on one important distinction. It is rarely quantity in itself which calls for criticism; more usually it is mediocrity, materialization, deviation or corruption. And here the root of the evil lies in spiritual indigence and the intrusion of impure grounds for action such as exist in the mind of sinful man. The danger proper to this particular tendency turns out to be that of risking the neglect of the essential in concentrating on some new addition. Dogma is neglected for new-fangled opinions, the revelation of the Gospel for private revelations or apparitions, faith for miracles and temporal favours, objective piety for subjective piety, the main structure of the liturgy for recently added feasts. Presbytery folk-lore tells a story about this which doubtless has its origin in *castigat ridendo mores* rather than in the strict truth. "Once upon a time, in a cathedral, the canons were reciting the Office. There was a sudden storm and the building was struck by lightning, setting fire to the tower. Faced by this danger, one of the canons pulled out his rosary and interrupted the recitation of the Office by saying: 'Brethren, let us pray!'" A caricature it is true, but one which illustrates very well a certain point of view in which fervour and merit are thought to begin only where obligation finishes.

Paradoxically, it is this very same outlook which drives those who hold it to try to get what corresponds to devotional attitudes made obligatory. This is why they try to promote new doctrinal definitions, and to obtain the condemnation of opinions which seem to them to be lacking in generosity. It explains their tendency to hold in reproach, if not to consider criminal, those who do not share with them some particular devotional form which is completely optional—to one of the apparitions for example. In this there is a misunderstanding of one of the first laws of devotion, the very essence of which is that it should be generosity of faith venturing out beyond the confines of defined dogma, and a practice going beyond what is obligatory. To want to extend the body of what is obligatory is to risk stifling this generous liberty or driving it into unbridled invention the continual renewal of which becomes essential to keep it alive. This tendency to set themselves up as judges and usurp the place of the Church's teaching authority springs from a leaning towards integrism and runs the risk of stifling by over-zealousness an important element in the life of Marian piety itself, freedom of spirit.

Those who hold the more critical view are right in keeping for the transcendence of Christ all the pre-eminence which it has by right; and for theology no less than for Marian devotion, their

78

purity, their balance and their proportions. They rightly draw attention to the existence of traditional theological criteria and to the importance of adjusting mariology to the rest of theology.

But those of this approach depart from right tradition when they hold back and adopt a negative attitude, and *a fortiori* when they show anger towards abuses and attack them without any mandate. If we take "integrism" as meaning "usurpation of judgment", then an integrist tendency can certainly be seen at work here in the actions of those who are not normally classed as integrists. This attitude is not consonant with the tradition of unreserved filial affection and unswerving attachment to the Virgin Mary which is professed by the Church. If their critical tendencies gain too firm a hold they will easily fall into a doctrinal insufficiency. Perfectly respectable forms of piety will no longer be understood or tolerated; devotions recommended by the Church, the rosary for example, and in extreme cases the whole Marian content of dogma, will be looked on with disfavour.

The issue will become even more complicated by a broad tendency to neglect *theologia* (that is, the deepening of fundamental dogmatic notions) in favour of a too exclusive attention to salvation history, that is, to *oeconomia*.

Finally, and this is something to which we shall return, ecumenical concern will exceed its proper limits and be given to all intents and purposes the value of a norm and criterion in dogmatic theology.

Fundamentally the best way of characterizing these two tendencies is to consider their extreme forms, those which they would and do take on when they are allowed to go to the farthest limit without restraint or opposition.

On one side, a state of poor-quality over-abundance would be reached turning Marian doctrine into a gnosis, and devotion to Mary into sectarianism and superstition; on the other, an icy purity from which irreproachable, doctrinal values as well as all devotion to Mary would have been eliminated.

In a word, corruption is the result on one side, emptiness on the other; the two tendencies, pushed to the extreme, both come to the same thing—nothing: the nothingness of incoherence and caricature in one case, the nothingness of impoverishment and iconoclasm in the other.

At the end of this analysis we are in a better position to understand that it is not a question of choosing between one or the
other of the alternatives, devotion or criticism, but rather a
question of two complementary tendencies which ought to complete and make up for each other's deficiencies. Each has its own
function; it is merely a matter of some adjustment and most of all
of enlightenment. The true equilibrium between them will come
about under the full light of doctrine and life.

We have touched on what may be the deepest cause of the
crisis affecting modern Marian theology and devotion, the dissociation of theology and life which has been widespread in all
the theology of the last few centuries. This fourth cause should
be added to those identified at the end of the preceding chapter.
It throws some light on them in retrospect. This is not the place
to investigate the date of the origin of this split. It was unknown
in Patristic times and in the Early Middle Ages, and would seem
to date in its beginnings from the thirteenth century. It grew up
as scholasticism became so increasingly absorbed in a completely
one-sided way in its rational labours that the vital sources and
orientation of theology of which St Thomas had always remained
so strongly aware were neglected. The deficiencies of this
theology—theoretical, abstract, inhuman—left the faithful hungry, and they looked for an answer to the problem on their own
ground, that of devotion, which thus began to flourish. Marian
piety was the chosen territory for these compensatory moves.
It was a reaction which in itself was normal and healthy, for life
had to go on. But the dissociation which was thus set up between
a purely theoretical theology and a poorly enlightened piety was
scarcely healthy. Spiritual forces which ought to have remained
harmoniously united (as we see them in the theology of Origen,
Augustine or Bernard) were suddenly pulled apart and thus left
open each to its own form of deviations—theology towards
rationalism, devotion towards a pietism justified basically in
what it was seeking for but always menaced by the danger of
over-materialization because of the lack of true spiritual knowledge. The type of mariology which flourished in the seventeenth
century only takes to itself the pietistic approaches and gives
them a theoretical form based on the exterior apparatus of
theology. This is no solution to our problem. Such an extravagant
type of theology is even more dangerous than the spontaneous

upsurges of piety which are in general humble and submissive to the authority of the Church. What is important is that theology should take more account of the specific nature of its object, which is a vital, saving truth, and that, in this spirit, it should make a place for the Blessed Virgin Mary who is so closely bound up with the very centre of the Mystery of Salvation.

IV

VIA AUREA

THE doctrinal and psychological analyses of the last chapter join up with the historical analysis and throw added light on the conclusions reached there. The differences of opinion to which Marian doctrine and piety have given rise (an abnormal phenomenon unknown in ancient times) must be attributed to an estrangement between properly correlative tendencies which then became exaggerated and corrupt. The way out will be found, not by making a choice between the two tendencies, but by separating out whatever is justified in their complementary emphases in order to attain a higher objectivity lying beyond each of them.

So as not to leave the reader in his perplexity for too long I made a beginning in the last chapter with an attempt at separating out the principle standards governing this discrimination and reconciliation.

All that remains now is to gather these conclusions together and bring them to completion. Once again, we shall examine the problem firstly from the doctrinal angle which conditions all the others, and then from the devotional and practical angle, which, in its turn, obeys its own criteria.

1. FINDING THE CENTRAL PEAK

If we look over the constituents of the two approaches which we have been examining in the preceding chapters, the conclusion to which we shall come is that the *Via Aurea* is in a sense a happy mean, provided that we understand this equivocal expression properly.

(1) It is not a matter of locating a mid-point equidistant between the two extremes, but a point of balance. No formula will enable us to fix this *a priori*. The centre of gravity of a balance may always be the true middle, but the same is not true of a lever. I mention this fact in order to dispel the facile illusion

which attempts to keep the balance between the two opinions in the very form in which they offer themselves to our attention. Such a method has the appearance of wisdom, but it is true to say that it is rather founded on laziness. It plays into the hands of the extremist by encouraging him in the stratagem of asking for the maximum so as to displace the centre of gravity of the debate to his own advantage.

(2) The golden mean in a matter like this cannot be a compromise or a levelling out of divergent demands; instead it must be like a central peak, just as the virtues are peaks midway between opposite vices—faith between credulity and unbelief, hope between despair and presumption, and so on. This is why the choice between the two outlooks sometimes appears as a choice in favour of one of them in which a valid emphasis against some particular corruption is found, sometimes as an adjustment, a search after a balanced position between the two opposing demands. This corresponds to the two aspects which must exist in a solution: it should, on the one hand, not fall below the required level, and, on the other, satisfy the complementary demands and emphases of each.

Because of this, we are led to keep various hierarchies of values very plainly in mind. Dogma should be preferred to hypothesis, the Gospel to private revelations, and in a general way, what is ancient and fundamental to what is new and subordinate.

We preferred commitment to indifference on the one hand, and *seeing* to *doing* on the other. But here the advantage recognized as existing on each side corresponds to the reconciliation of complementary demands—involvement and objectivity. The same applied when we condemned one side for its tendency to disregard the transcendence of God, and the other for failing to appreciate the transforming immanence of his grace. The equilibrium in Marian theology is again found at the central peak where the two sets of complementary demands culminate.

Various pairs of ideas must be adjusted and co-ordinated in this way—the apprehension of the mystery with the investigation of the sources, the logical elaboration and the perspective of salvation history, the logic of what is appropriate and the gratuity of Mary's destiny, personalism and intellectual abstraction,[1] the analogies and the differences between Christ and Mary on the one hand, and between Mary and the rest of redeemed humanity on the other.

This search for a balanced position between two complementary lines of approach will be essentially a search for *meaning* in the setting of a wisdom in which *theologia* and *oeconomia*, the values of truth and the values of life, will find that harmony which is so necessary and which modern theology has so unhappily divided. Each truth will be situated in its double connection with the general pattern of the whole of dogma and with "the last end of man". Such a procedure will avoid both turning mariology into a closed discipline and also impoverishing it or emptying it of its full meaning.

Thus, the divine motherhood has primarily and principally a christological significance in connection with the Incarnation and the wide scheme of the mystery of salvation. Secondarily, but inseparably from this, it has a significance with regard to Mary, as the object of God's predilection, filled to overflowing with his redeeming grace, and witness thereby to the transforming power of the gift of God. Finally, following this same line of thought, it has a value in connection with the life of grace in each of us, as an exemplar, in virtue of our special link with the highest member of the mystical body. This corresponds with the two complementary aspects of Mary's role: she attracts us as a model, she is present in Christ as a mother.

In the same way Mary's virginity finds its fundamental significance in its relation to the mystery of Christ. At the very beginning of the work of salvation it is established as a witness to the transcendence of God's gift, to the Son of God conceived in this way. This is why the Fathers, as we said above, saw in it above all else the specific sign of the Incarnation. Correlatively Mary's virginity is the prototype of Christian virginity. It opens the way for those who answer Christ's invitation: "If you would be perfect . . ." (Matt. 19. 21), and who, by the total renunciation of the world and the flesh, bear witness to the absolute sufficiency of God and to the eschatological goal of the destiny to which he is leading us: that eternity in which all the biological functions of this world are left behind, where "they will no longer marry or be given in marriage", as Christ said (Matt. 22. 30), and where "God will be all in all" (1 Cor. 15. 28).

In brief, the general picture and the details of Marian theology have a meaning both as regards God and as regards us, and this implies something which has been fulfilled in the person of Mary herself, and which is normally called "her privileges". What goes to make up her glory must also be examined. But this glory is in no way increased—rather the opposite—if we forget the double functional meaning of Mary, both as regards Christ and as regards the Church, for it is precisely in this that the degree and importance of her glory lie.

This attempt to put Mary in her correct position and setting can perhaps be illuminated by a maxim in which is contained a balancing factor which helps to get things into their right proportions:

> *Mary is totally relative to God;*
> *Mary is totally correlative to the Church.*

It is perhaps better to make absolutely clear, although it should go without saying, that she is both these things *in Christ, through Christ and for Christ.*

The first of these two principles was perfectly expounded by the French School from Bérulle to Grignion de Montfort. It was one of the factors making for the essential soundness in this whole line of writers at a time when balance was particularly lacking. To be more precise, Mary in being relative to God is fundamentally and immediately relative to Christ. It is a relation of total dependence which makes her completely God's with no reserve and no exception, withholding nothing, unlike the rest of humanity. Thus she is a sign in which we are shown God. By all that she is and does she tends to lead us to Christ.

The slight nuance in the second half of the formula will have been noticed; the term *correlative* is used in place of *relative* in relation to the Church, for Mary is not in a state of mere dependence in relation to the Church as she is in relation to God. She is, in the plan of salvation, the figure and the prototype of the Church which is itself also completely relative to God. We are thus dealing with a correlation in which Mary is first in the chronological order, in the sense that she came before the Church of Pentecost (Luke 1. 35 and Acts 1. 8), and in the ontological order, in the sense that in her there is concentrated, as in a supreme example, all that the grace of God brings about in the

Church. This does not prevent her being a member of it. Did she not receive from it the word and the sacraments which sustained the last years of her earthly life? This correlation, therefore, does not imply a mere parallelism as of two completely separate or independent realities, but a dependence and a kind of inclusion in each other. Mary and the Church both show the same fundamental connection with Christ, an identical type of relation implying an identical life. In this Mary comes first as the one who sets up the relation of Christ with humanity, and thereby with the Church, but the ultimate finality is, nevertheless, the Church in which is made present the salvation of men for whom Christ "was incarnate in the womb of the Virgin Mary".

It is very important to safeguard the meaning of this double relationship of Mary to Christ and to the Church. One of the principal indications of the mariological crisis of the present day is that it has been possible for men to set the christological and the ecclesiological tendencies against each other as if they were two inimical and opposite views, and that it has been possible to see one as an endeavour to separate Mary from the Church, and the other as a subversive attempt to "separate Mary from Christ". Those who can grasp correctly the inseparable nature of the double correlation which has just been set out will find no sense at all in any such antithesis.

2. RESPECT FOR THE LIMITS

The search for the central peak will be carried on in a more lucid fashion if the frontiers beyond which Marian theology should not attempt to go are kept in mind. Six limits show up clearly the difference between the Virgin Mary and Christ.

The first and most obvious of these is that she is not God but simply a creature. Differing in this from Christ, she is not a divine person, but simply a human person. By virtue of this, her presence in the Church is not of the same order as his divine presence.

The second is that, unlike Christ, she was redeemed. This solid fact was for a long time a serious obstacle to the definition of the Immaculate Conception, and the dogma could only be defined when this particular truth had been explicitly integrated with it. Under these two headings Mary is completely dependent on

86

Christ who himself acts with his own sovereign power. She has neither privileges, nor any co-operation in salvation, nor "mediation" except in him and through him.

The following three points concern the strictly temporal character of Mary's destiny as against the destiny of Christ. Jesus' personal eternity extends beyond his human existence. The Word pre-exists, but Mary did not exist before the moment of her conception. According to the commonly accepted doctrine, Christ possessed the beatific vision, while Mary made her earthly pilgrimage in the obscurity of faith, blessed because she believed (Luke 1. 45). Christ did not have to merit his own salvation, for in his own person he was God; Mary had to merit hers in all humility.

Finally, Mary is a woman and because of this is excluded from some of the hierarchical characters and functions which are reserved for those of the male sex. The mission of officially representing Christ, acting in his name, delivering with authority the word of salvation to men, together with the precepts and sacraments which guide and nourish the Church was never hers.

To say all this is perhaps to emphasize the obvious. It all goes without saying, and yet saying it does have a good effect. It is hard to imagine to what extent these limits have taxed the ingenuity of the devotees of Mary, who, irritated by them, have tried to push them further back.

Thus they have given her in a metaphorical sense the title of goddess (Marracci collected quite a number of examples of this),[2] or even called her "the fourth person of the Trinity".[3] But such bizarre ideas are out of fashion now and are generally to be found in non-theological literature. Let's leave the dead to bury the dead.

That Mary was redeemed is a fact which still upsets some mariologists today. The ardour with which some fight against all idea of a *debitum* be it *proximum* or *remotum* tends to weaken the concept.[4]

The temptation to accord to Mary some sort of pre-existence is much less common. The poetical metaphors which occur frequently in the liturgy applying texts which in fact refer to the real pre-existence of the Word (Prov. 8. 22-36) to her eternal predestination, sometimes raise questions and inspire dreams in insufficiently enlightened minds. This is a problem that has been set me more than once and I have in my library an essay recently printed *pro manuscripto* which went so far as positively to defend her pre-existence. It is an isolated attempt and has not been followed up.

Attempts to overcome the last two limits are more frequent. These limits are much less of a restraint dogmatically and yet they are very important for the proper significance of the role of Mary.

Numerous authors accord the beatific vision to Mary during her earthly life. We shall consider the difficulties of this opinion later.

Others have tried to attribute to her a priesthood of a hierarchical type and a royalty including a true dominion together with the effective exercise of kingly power of the same kind as Christ's.

There are two reasons for directing attention to these limits. First of all, they put in a clear light the transcendence of the Saviour and his role as chief, and, furthermore, the distinction between Christ and Mary. At the same time, they demonstrate the positive significance of Mary's role in her relation to Christ. It is also good to remember that a creature, one who has been redeemed and lives by faith, should have been called to so intimate a participation, passive and active, in the divine redemption. It is just as good to remember that Mary is the summit and supreme model of the Church in its life of faith. Similarly it is good to remember that her grace is displayed without exception under the conditioning of her womanhood. Doubtless God could, *in theory*, have given to his mother, even if it were as an exception, the hierarchical functions and privileges of the apostles. He did not do so, and this fact is surely full of meaning, even though we still have some difficulty in formulating the reason for it exactly (cf. 1 Cor. 11. 3-9).

The corollary of this is that it is important to make clear both in the conceptual framework and in terminology, the distinction between Mary and Christ. The meaning and the formulation of this differentiation have progressed through various stages in theology Thus, for example, the expression: "to worship the Virgin Mary" was still in current use in the seventeenth century.[5] The sense in which the writers of that period understood it was perfectly valid. Worship was (and still is) a generic word which covers both the worship of *latria* which is reserved for God alone, and the worship of *dulia* which is given to the saints. When it was necessary to be explicit, the above distinction was made clear, but these technical terms never got into the language of ordinary people in which the term *worship* has come to be reserved for God, while for Mary and the saints *honour* and *venerate* have been the more usual words. This evolution in terminology is a happy one, for it sets off well the divine transcendence without in any way detracting from the devotion due to the saints. It effectively gets rid of any risk of imprecision or misreading and of any uneasiness in the use of words. The seventeenth-century apologists gave a good example by not clinging to the use of the term "worship", even though it might have been perfectly justified in a given conceptual system. Normally the tendency among mariologists is just the opposite, as we have seen; they love to elaborate terms which confuse Christ and Mary under one denomination. This path does not lead to a balanced view.

Since we are here concerned with finding such a path, and not with setting up one-sided rules, it should be added that it will also be a good thing not to confuse Mary and the rest of redeemed humanity under the same terms. Curiously enough, it is sometimes the reaction of certain theologians to a one-sided assimilation of Mary to Christ, to assimilate her to all Christians. They see this as a means of moderating the process which tends to take the Virgin Mary away from the rest of the faithful by making her pass over victoriously to the side of Christ They say that if Mary is mediatrix, all Christians are mediators. If Mary is co-redemptrix, all Christians are co-redeemers, because of their active participation in the work of Redemption. Mary is joined to the hypostatic order because of her divine motherhood; but all Christians are so joined in so far as they are, through the baptismal character, members of the mystical body of which a divine Person is the head. And so on.

To sum up, what is generally desirable is such a terminology and an organization of concepts as will show clearly not only Mary's resemblances to Christ, on the one hand, and to Christians on the other, but also the differences between each of them and her. Above all, the hierarchy of these resemblances and differences, which all take their root in Christ, must not be forgotten, nor their significance in relation to the transcendence of God and the salvation of man.

3. RESPECT FOR CRITERIA

Although it is much more technical and theoretically much more obvious, one last rule must be set out. Mariology must respect throughout the traditional criteria of theology and any other accessory disciplines it may use.

This principle suffers from a threefold difficulty.

In the first place, mariology brings into play an amazing number of very varied disciplines: exegesis, patristics, mediaeval and modern thought, hymnology and iconography (this last has been badly neglected). Then there are the speculative processes by which theology makes the intelligibility of its object clear. It is impossible for any one man to be really qualified in all of them. But the mariologist must at least know of their existence, and have some idea of the proper demands of each, so as not to violate their standards. Mariologists have, on the whole, a bad reputation for "scientific" work in spite of their efforts to pursue it correctly, efforts which have more than once been crowned with success. This comes from the fact that, since mariology is not really a specialized field of study characterized by its own specific technique, they have to hunt about everywhere and, unfortunately, at times to poach! Mariology needs, in the first place, a standard of culture, of openness and of humility.

In the second place, as we have already seen, by specializing, mariology has tended to become cut off from theology and to break loose from it, to establish its own standards of approach, while theologians have tended to lose interest in mariology although it is intrinsically a proper concern of theirs.

In the third place, there has been a crisis concerning criteria in our time, from which we have not yet emerged completely, in spite of the readjustments which the confrontations of the Council have brought about.

Broadly speaking, the crisis sprang from the following fact. While specialists were going ahead with the study of Scripture and the Fathers on their own, textbook theology, and even, indeed, official theology, showed no particular fondness for either, and in fact gave signs of outright suspicion of them. The tendency was to be satisfied with a teaching authority which, as it had been raised to the dignity of a third source, did away with any need to have recourse to the other two. This failure to remember the close living link between the teaching authority (the "proximate standard") and the sources (the fundamental standard from which the authority draws its inspiration and to which it submits) was very harmful to the healthy conduct of theological studies. Opinions born in the nineteenth century and spread abroad in the manuals of theology tended to pass as "the traditional doctrine", while some of the greatest patristic theses fell out of favour, and the modern evolution of doctrine tended to class as outdated or erroneous doctrines which had held a place of honour among the Fathers and Doctors of the Church. Mariology suffered particularly from this situation. Though it owed its birth as theology to a piety opposed to a dry-as-dust rationalistic sort of theology, mariology itself has often fallen into the same kind of rationalism whenever it has tried to become "scientific". It lacked, and to some extent it still lacks, in many ways the benefit of a solid foundation, and it is because of this that it is so easily led astray into the evolutive and particularizing paths which so disfigure it.

This is not the place to go into the whole question of dogmatic criteria. We can only mention certain points which have a particular bearing on the healthy development of Marian theology.

The investigation of sources

First of all comes foundation upon and good use of sources. Just as for all other theology, so also for mariology its one concern is the understanding and explanation of the Revelation given once for all.

The foundation must first be scriptural, for the Scriptures have God as their author, and in them we have his very word. They possess for this reason an unequalled dignity, and it is the classical teaching of St Thomas that all that is essential is found in substance in them.[6]

One must, therefore, be on one's guard against the unhappy notion which has been current in mariology since the sixteenth century, that Scripture is silent on the subject of Mary, a prejudice which has given rise to a proliferation of parascriptural doctrines. The inverse error which would *per fas et nefas* find everything explicitly in Scripture must be avoided just as much. The foundations of the doctrines of the Assumption and the Immaculate Conception, for example, are to be found there, but the doctrines themselves are not formally indicated.

Mariologists must not forget in their zeal that there is a "highway code" in exegesis. Those who do not observe it rigorously are disqualified and go astray. It is particularly useful to remember, with the encyclical *Divino Afflante*, the primacy of the literal sense over the secondary or derived senses (the typical or figurative sense, the plenary sense and, most of all, the accommodated sense).

This code of Catholic exegesis answers to the general rules of all hermeneutics and should never violate them. It has in addition its own rules: Scripture is linked to Tradition, and is itself an object of tradition (*tradita ab Ecclesia*—handed down by the Church). The Church delivers to us and transmits (in Latin *tradit*) to us an attitude towards the sacred text, a manner of apprehending it and of understanding it, a sense of the relative importance of the whole and of particular details, and of the relation of particular parts to each other, and, in certain cases, even the precise meaning of a given text.

The use of Tradition is thus complementary to that of Scripture, but presents a more delicate problem. This is so, because the *object* of Tradition properly so called is presented to us closely mingled with an extremely complex mass of writings, monuments and practices. Thus it is found to be mixed up with many inauthentic traditions and opinions. This situation warns us not to confuse the history of doctrines, and even less the compilation of what are simply catalogues of texts, with positive theology which has as its object the discernment of the true *content of revelation* transmitted as a normative standard in the midst of this complexity. Such discrimination will help us to avoid confusing Tradition with a capital T with the little esoteric traditions of recent date and no authority, which are too easily held in honour among mariologists.

In this work it is essential to safeguard the true scale of values, in antiquity and authority recognized by the Church. It is very necessary to remember in this context the importance of the

Greek Fathers (systematic bibliographies show just how much mariology has neglected them), and also of iconography in the extent in which it is a vehicle expressing the faith and prayer of the Church.

What place should be given in this to the *sensus fidelium*?

This idea presents some delicate problems and paradoxes. Those of the Reformed Churches, for example, give great weight to the doctrinal activity of the whole Christian people, yet they have completely scorned the value of this witness when it has had to do with the Blessed Virgin. On the contrary, Catholicism, and precisely the most rigid elements in it, those that are most minimalist when it comes to conceding any value to the laity and anything originating from them, exalt the *sensus fidelium* to the skies the moment they have to deal with Marian theology. Sometimes it is turned into a veritable panacea. The *sensus fidelium* takes the place of argument in matters where such is lacking. There are times when the theologian who uses it to weight the balance is referring only to an opinion current in his own country or his own parish, or even to what is nothing but his own personal opinion.

What, first of all, is this *sensus fidelium*? It is the faith of the whole body of Christians, indefectibly preserved in the Church by the Holy Spirit. There the most radical infallibility of the Church lies, its living infallibility (*in credendo*), correlative to the infallibility of the teaching Church (*in docendo*), which is the infallibility of the whole body of bishops culminating in the visible head of the Church. But, while this supreme teaching authority can formulate precise definitions, the *sensus fidelium* is something more diffuse. Nothing is more difficult than trying to grasp among an ill-defined mass of manifestations, of which some are authentic and others not, this *sensus* of which the Holy Spirit assures the infallibility, not to each believer, but to the whole of the Church. To discern it demands a tremendous amount of work. Above all it demands a special approach, and it is most important that the method of this approach should be brought to perfection. Often the method used to discern the nature of the *sensus fidelium* is as approximate as the way some men diagnose "current opinion" from nothing but a simple impression founded on one or two striking facts. Those who have perfected and use methods of obtaining the trends of opinion are less naïvely confident and more modest in their claims. We might do worse than take their method of work, together with their modesty, as an example, when it comes to exploring the evidence of this *sensus* in a restricted or universal collectivity, without, of course, doing anything which would prejudice the criteria proper to theology.

In any case, it is important to underline the fact that this *sensus fidelium* is not the opinion of the "laity" as separate from the clergy, nor of the "people" as different from the hierarchy. It is the *sensus* of all believers. Furthermore, there is nothing which permits us to say that it has any more value in mariology than in other fields of theology. If it is agreed that it has played a determinative role there, then the rightness of this still remains to be proved. If the value it has been given is justified, it does not follow from this that it ought to play the same guiding role in the future. And even if it were called to do so, the artificial stimulation of propaganda and vast petitions drawn up on the spur of the moment would not be the best way to encourage its purest manifestation, which comes from the Holy Spirit.

Marian theology, like all forms of theology, must give a place of the first order to the teaching authority or magisterium of the Church which is the most immediate standard of faith, since it was to the apostles and their successors that Christ said: "Go and teach all nations. . . . Whoever shall believe and be baptized shall be saved" (Matt. 28. 19; Mark 16. 16), and again: "He who hears you hears me, he who despises you despises me" (Luke 10. 16).

The complexity in which we find this standard clothed is in some ways greater than that of Scripture, in the sense that Scripture is *inspired* by the Spirit, and the magisterium only *assisted* by the Spirit. Thus Scripture is formally the *Word of God*, whereas the acts of the magisterium cannot claim this dignity. Nevertheless, this standard is a more immediate one, in the sense that its function is the discernment, in the last resort, of the content of Scripture and Tradition, and the infallible definition of this when the need arises.

Theology must, therefore, safeguard the true import of this living link between the magisterium and the sources of the faith. Any work which is to be fruitful in achieving this must be more than a mere one-sided study, either of the magisterium or of the sources. Rather it must be the interpretation of the magisterium in the light of all the sources and *vice versa*. Study of the acts of the magisterium will permit an appraisal of the value and true meaning of the sources; that of the sources, an extension and proper situation of the affirmations of the magisterium which do not claim to be complete, but only to define certain important facts as has seemed necessary for the Church in particular circumstances. To undertake this comparison is a difficult task, demanding great effort and perseverance, but it is of first-rate importance. By it, unexpected details are brought into relief, rather in the way they appear when the two images in a stereoscope are brought into focus. Negatively, however, the naïve way in which some people try to project the decisions of the magisterium into ancient texts and try to see, for example, in the works of the African Fathers some of the mariological theses which have appeared in the encyclicals of the last few centuries, is as foolish as the ancient belief that all the branches and leaves of an oak tree were already materially distinct in the acorn from which it sprang. Such procedures do nothing to increase the honour in which the magisterium is held; rather do they lower it.

Furthermore, the authority of the magisterium is not so monolithic and does not speak with so single a voice as our desire for simplification and clean lines would lead some into thinking. There is a one-sided way of interpreting papal texts that leads to the paradoxical position where the proof for different and opposing theories is drawn by the partisans of each from the same texts. So, some maintain that the authority of certain encyclicals guarantees the doctrine of "objective co-redemption", others that this is not the case. Some assert that the Constitution *Munificentissimus* supports the view that Mary did in fact die, others that its witness is rather to her immortality, whereas Pius XII merely had the intention of not becoming embroiled on either side in this question. Such goings-on show little respect for the light which the magisterium can throw on problems, but rather obscure it. So it is very important that we should have a thorough grasp of the distinctions which must be made in these matters of interpretation.

First, papal magisterium must be distinguished from episcopal. The latter has been very much neglected, and this has done great harm, for Christ's words did not confine doctrinal authority to Peter alone, but to Peter on the one hand (Matt. 16. 19), and to the whole of the apostolic college on the other (Matt. 18. 18). When a bishop exercises his office as teacher, this has more than a merely local value. It has a meaning for the whole Church. A more subtle, yet no less important, distinction brought back and given its true value once again by John XXIII is that between the magisterial acts of the pope as head of the universal Church and those which he performs as bishop of the diocese of Rome (between these two extremes could be added his acts as archbishop, as Primate of Italy, or as Patriarch of the West, in the matter of the *Latin* liturgy for instance). Thus, the moderating counsels of John XXIII on the subject of Marian devotion were given by him not for the universal Church, for there are many countries for which they would have no point, but in view of the needs of his own diocese.

In the second place, not all the acts of the Holy See have the same authority. The range is considerable. At the top come the definitions of the faith properly so called which are very exceptional. There have been only two concerned with Marian matters since the foundation of the Church (1854 and 1950). Next to these comes a whole gamut of degrees, forms and nuances: disciplinary or doctrinal documents of a more or less solemn nature and dealing with matters of greater or less importance, addressed to the whole Church, or to more or less restricted groups, nations, provinces, national or international congresses, big or small pilgrimages to Rome. Equally important from the point of view of magisterial authority is the distinction between acts signed by the pope, those communicated in his name, and those published by the many different organs of the Holy See in virtue of the habitual authority conferred on them by the papacy.

We must also underline the distinction between the extraordinary magisterium in which papal infallibility is formally and explicitly at stake, and the *ordinary* magisterium. Before the middle of the nineteenth century some theologians used the term "extended magisterium", since the documents included under this heading are not drawn up as a strict expression of a standard, but rather have such an effect more or less diffused through them. A new and significant characteristic of recent doctrinal documents is the way in which they so readily take the form, not of an enunciation of dogma on a particular critical point, but of a wide-ranging exposition on a whole topic in which the intentions appear with all sorts of nuances, from the clearest to the most discreet, doctrinal decisions or strict disciplinary prescriptions, directives, invitations and insinuations. In this respect, the importance which encyclicals have taken on is very characteristic.

In brief, the magisterium is the most immediate standard, but its documents have a normative character that may vary greatly, and the evaluation of the standard calls for an exegetical effort which can come only from an open mind, and the observation of precise and complex rules. Some of these are old and permanent. Thus, as an example, the authority of a doctrinal document attains essentially the decision promulgated in the document. The chief function of the reasons adduced is to explain the decision, to make clear why it was taken and to commend its acceptance. In the same way, if the pope quotes a text in an encyclical, he does not by so doing normally mean to authenticate a particular exegesis of the text in question, and his authority resides far less in these quotations (which can be simply illustrations for the document) than in those passages in which he speaks by his own authority. Thus Pius XII carefully avoided any expression which might suggest the death of Mary in the drafting of the Bull defining the Assumption of the Blessed Virgin, but he inserted texts from Tradition among which certain spoke of her death, in order not to put out of court that tradition which, nevertheless, he did not intend to consecrate with his own authority. Another important rule is that when a pontifical document seems to go contrary to an opinion received by the Fathers or Doctors of the Church, notably by such a one as St Thomas Aquinas, this doctrine should not be thought to be rejected by it, unless the papal document says so in so many words.

Finally, the literary genre of the various documents must not be forgotten. The use of this distinction, which has been current for long now in biblical exegesis, has aroused a certain amount of dislike in connection with its use in the exegesis of the acts of the magisterium. It has been applied with hesitation, even with repugnance. There has been an obscure fear that its use would undermine the authority of the documents in question. But the comparison of the different styles proper to different documents and different popes forces it on us, particularly where they approach the same problems or analogous problems with different nuances. For a notable example compare the decree *Ineffabilis Deus* defining the Immaculate Conception with *Munificentissimus* which contains the definition of the Assumption. This idea, like all others, is open to abuse but, whether we like it or not, all human literary activity belongs to some particular genre. There is no possible way of escaping from this! Every literary composition has necessarily a characteristic literary form. It is, admittedly, an important characteristic of papal documents that they abstain, as far as is possible, from expressions or considerations of a personal, private or disputable nature and stick to what is most essential and least ephemeral. Their style is solemn and studied and shorn of all trace of fantasy. These characteristics are none the less those of a particular literary form which is easily recognizable, and which would enable anyone to identify an encyclical simply by reading a few pages taken at random.

In addition to these fundamental characteristics, there are others which are determined by the subject itself or by the personality of the pontiff. For example, the renewal that John XXIII brought to this literary form is particularly striking in the documents with which he was himself closely identified and which will remain the mark of his pontificate. He was, for instance, concerned less to define clear, precise notions or to enunciate logically and systematically ordered principles, than to point out key ideas, vital notions which he wished to see taken up throughout the Church, or again, distinctions of a rather approximate nature which might help to open the way to further research. Such were his famous distinctions between the "substance" of a dogma and its "notional expression", and then also between "doctrine" and "movements" in the practical field.

This question of literary forms is of particular importance in Marian theology. For lack of an enlightened method of exegesis, papal teaching is interpreted in the most varied and conflicting ways in different types of mariology, as one goes from one school of thought to another. This lack of method constitutes a real drawback because it creates uncertainties and confusion in men's minds about the magisterium itself. A not too recent example may be quoted, from the times when the popes themselves signed letters of thanks to authors who had sent them complimentary copies of their works. In a letter to Mgr Van den Berghe, the author of a book on the Marian priesthood, Pius IX wrote: "The Mother of God . . . is so closely united to the sacrifice of her divine Son that she has been called the *Virgin Priest* by the Fathers of the Church." Certain partisans of the Marian priesthood were overjoyed at these words, seeing them as the seal of the "infallible pope" on the doctrine. It was indeed the infallible pope who signed the document in question, but it was a document which in no way involved his infallibility, particularly in a section which was an illustration with no normative value. What is more, it is a fact that no Father of the Church ever used the expression "Virgin Priest"!

The most widely misunderstood consideration in this connection is that the majority of the Marian documents issued by the papal magisterium in the last century have had to do with devotional matters, notably with the rosary. Though they may indeed contain important doctrinal considerations destined to enlighten the devotion of the faithful, they are not, for all that, dogmatic constitutions. The intention behind them is not so much to define a body of doctrine as to bring forward considerations calculated to nourish and enlighten devotional fervour. For this reason their style is better classed as homiletic, and their language tends to be oratorical, full of images, and sometimes more generous than rigorous. The intention is to move and to arouse, not to further opinions or to settle quarrels between different schools of thought. It would be a bad mistake if one were to take pastoral utterances of this kind and turn them into dogmatic theses.

For example, Benedict XV declared that Mary "abdicated her maternal rights over her Son for the sake of the salvation of the world". This is a metaphorical expression and not a strict definition of the close bonds of mutual belonging on a moral and emotional level which normally exist between a mother and her son. If a man gives his life for his country, and his mother approves of his conduct or openly supports him in his sacrifice, it could not be said in any strict sense, but only in a poetic or epic sense, that she had "abdicated her rights", for she has no strict rights over the *person* of her son. There is nothing which can authorize her to hinder her son in his decision to sacrifice his life, and the son would be in no way obliged to obey her if she did decide to do so.[7] Benedict XV added that Mary sacrificed (*immolavit*) her Son in so real a way that it is perfectly justifiable to say that she herself redeemed the human race with Christ (*humanum genus redemisse*). The term *sacrificed* is obviously metaphorical : it was first introduced by pious authors who were trying to promote the doctrine of the sacrificial priesthood of Mary, a doctrine which received a very cool welcome indeed from the Church. The term throws into striking relief the intimate, active, painful and selfless communion of Mary in the sacrifice of her Son. The expression can be accepted, but this does not mean that the words must be taken in their strict sense. "Generosity" with the use of vocabulary is here in control and this is a very typical echo of the Italian piety of the age. Because of this we shall know how to treat the end of the sentence according to which Mary "redeemed the human race". What must be retained of what these words express is the fact that there was a certain degree of co-operation on the part of Mary in the work of redemption, but no precise help can be drawn from them in seeking a solution to the problem set by the specialists as to whether Mary co-operated in the objective redemption or the subjective redemption. As we said already, Pius XII, who had reflected very deeply on the Marian question in general and on this problem in particular, was of the opinion at the end of his life that it had not yet been settled and was not yet ripe for definitive solution.

Theological reflection and systematization

If the first stage of all scientific theology is the examination of the sources, the second consists in making clear the understanding of the mystery, and finding a synthetic formulation which will separate from the multiplicity of the sources the simplicity of the divine thought in so far as this is accessible to our human minds.

At this stage of the work the mariologist should not give in to the illusion that mariology springs from its own special principles, like a plant from its seed. St Thomas Aquinas puts a very different view before us. The article of the *Summa* which is *ex professo* devoted to the question of principles in theology[8] in turn considers two meanings of this expression.

The principles of theology for him are, first of all, the facts of Revelation transmitted by Scripture and Tradition, and secondly, and this may seem more surprising, the knowledge of the blessed, that is to say, the perfect knowledge of himself which God gives to the saints in heaven, according to a mode which is both human and divine. Theology is subordinate to this blessed science, states St Thomas, somewhat as "perspective" is to "geometry" from which it draws all its principles. This second sense, which is less technical and more mystical, may seem to be less strict. It is important, for it shows, on the one hand, the mission of theology —to explain the thought of God in terms of the human mind, translating it into terrestrial language—and, on the other hand, the humble condition of this science, depending, as it does, on a vision which is very elusive and which will never be adequate for its object. It makes us think of a blind man learning the names of the colours and the shapes of various objects before an operation by which he hopes to gain his sight.

These two senses of the word "principle" apply to the case of mariology quite naturally in precisely the same way as they apply to the rest of theology of which mariology is an integral part. St Thomas envisages only these two senses in the preliminary article of the *Summa* which we have just summarized. Elsewhere he gives explicit consideration to a third sense, in which the principles of theology are the *articles of faith*, that is to say, the principal propositions of the Creed in which all the essential points of revelation are formulated.[9] In this sense Marian theology has no principles proper to itself; it is an integral part of the article in the Creed which concerns the Incarnation: ". . . born of the Virgin Mary". It is also involved in other articles: that concerning Christ's passion and death, because of Mary's presence on Calvary; that concerning the resurrection of the body, because of her Assumption; and so on.

But none of this corresponds exactly[10] to the "principles of Marian theology" held in such honour among mariologists. Perhaps, then, these should be challenged in the name of St Thomas? The answer to this lies in the fact that the great Doctor himself uses principles of this kind, without, however, giving us his theory on them. These are *synthetic principles,* the formal function of which is to make clear the intelligibility of a revealed doctrine, to enable it to be grasped in a deeper and more unified fashion, to set it out in a coherent order from its central facts to its last and most developed consequence. This is a characteristic trait of his speculative method. So, for example, as he treats of each of the theological virtues, he starts by defining its object: the truth of God as far as faith is concerned, his power for hope, his goodness for charity; and it is from these starting-points that he resolves the particular questions of detail. In the same way, the treatise on the Trinity, one of the most remarkable and most unified in the *Summa Theologica*, throws light on all the questions involved, by starting from the equation *person = relationship*. This identification made at the start helps to safeguard in a very enlightening way the absolute unity of the divine essence (*esse in*) in which all is one and identical, except where there is an opposition of relationship (*esse ad*).

These principles of systematization are nothing but the rational formulation of a key truth implicit in the sources of theology (St Thomas devoted a very large part of his efforts to the exploration of these). This truth may help to set out the unity, coherence and interconnection of each question considered, and St Thomas follows up the consequences rigorously; but even so he never loses contact with the sources, on the one hand, and the last end and complete life of man on the other. (Vatican I, by the way, very opportunely recalled the fundamental importance of this last consideration for the understanding of the faith —*De fide*, c. 4, Denzinger, 1796.) The systematic work of the theologian must be something more than a pure deduction starting from an abstract principle; it is a synthetic formulation of scattered and complex data in which nothing may be altered or diminished, and, what is more, of a mystery which will never be adequately expressed in human language.

Therefore, we must distinguish between two types of principle in current use in Marian theology.

In the first place, there is the formulation (still under discussion) of the key point of revelation in what concerns Mary, broadly speaking the divine motherhood, to which as to a central fundamental truth all the other data concerning the Virgin Mary can be attached. This has an undeniable theological consistency, answering as it does to the single article of the Creed in which she is explicitly mentioned. In this application the word principle covers an object of faith properly so called.

Of less value are the other principles, which consist simply in general maxims offering possibilities for deductions about various matters.

Thus there are the principles known as the principles of singularity, of pre-eminence, and of resemblance to Christ. These are the products of induction from the perception, after the deepening of the understanding of many questions over the course of centuries, that in each field the Virgin Mary showed special privileges, *eminent* particularities which are proper to her and put her in a position of particular closeness to Christ. These principles do, indeed, correspond to truths, but a systematic application of them must be guarded against. They come far short of being universally valid in every circumstance and every particular case. Their limits must be carefully delineated. This could lead to the formulation of complementary or compensatory principles, perhaps even of counter-principles. Thus the "singularity" and the "pre-eminence" which characterize the Virgin Mary have as their starting-point her fundamental resemblance to all other humans, to all the rest of the redeemed. It is of some interest to set out this particular principle, wording it, perhaps, as follows: the Virgin Mary has all the specific characteristics of human nature identically with all other human beings. She has the specific characteristics of femininity, like any other woman. Though the grace which is hers is of an unequalled fullness, it is still of the same kind as the grace which comes to the rest of redeemed humanity; it is a similar participation in the being and the very life of God; it is expressed in the same theological virtues. And all of this comes in Mary, as in everyone else, from the free gift of God.

Analogous limitations must be laid down in connection with the well-known principle of suitability: *"potuit, decuit, ergo fecit"* (God was able, it was fitting, therefore he did it). In other words, it was in the power of God to grant to Mary some particular exemption from the general rule; such an exemption was consonant with the honour of God and the glory of Mary; in his wisdom he, therefore, made this exemption. This kind of reasoning did great service in helping theologians to get out of the impasse in which almost all of them found themselves caught in the thirteenth century on the subject of the first "sanctification" of Mary. This success in a case which was both difficult and of long standing gave this principle its extraordinary fame. This does not make systematic applications of it any the less dangerous; it would lead, with the best intentions in the world, to a surfeit of useless jewels in Mary's crown! Certain inventions of the seventeenth-century authors call to mind those Roman Madonnas which were often seriously damaged—the top of the head being cut off—in order that they might be crowned. A coronation can be not only an unnecessary extravagance, but also a mutilation. Thus, if we attribute to Mary the beatific vision during her earthly life, we at once remove her from the life of faith which is one of the sources of her merit. At the same time, her value as the supreme example and as the summit of the faith of the Church is spoiled. That which is the crown of her true beatitude according to Scripture is taken from her: "Blessed is she who has believed" (Luke 1. 45). What is fitting in the eyes of men, even of holy and sincere men, is not always so in the eyes of God, for his thoughts are not our thoughts and his ways are not our ways. In the Bible, as in the conduct of events in the world and in our own lives, his wisdom is often disconcerting and baffling to us. It is not possible to reduce it to a closed system in which all his actions could be foreseen.

It is very important that Marian theology should become more aware of the purely relative nature of its principles of systematization, of their limits, of their subordination to the sources, and of the transcendence of God's thought. Even if it is, of necessity, an exercise of the intelligence and rightly has a rational aspect, theology, nevertheless, cannot be detached from the order of analogy and mystery; it is inadequate by its very nature, and must, therefore, beware of the temptation to rationalism. Experience shows how this takes hold of theologians and can point out only too well the ravages it causes. The Church has already had to condemn those who made the existence of God an immediate evidence to the reason (ontologism) and who made of the Trinity a logical theorem or an inevitable deduction. Who can say *a priori* how it was fitting for God to proportion in Mary glory and humility, affliction and sweetness, life in communion with him or separated from him?

In Marian theology, one of the processes in which the rationalist temptation is most clearly revealed—and one of the most common—is that in which the reasoning proceeds as follows:

such and such a word necessarily implies such and such a meaning, and not to recognize this full meaning would be to reduce dogma to sheer nominalism. Thus they would say, for example, that Mary, as dogma assures us, is the Mother of God; now, she would not really be the Mother of God but only mother of a man if she were not the instrumental cause of the Incarnation itself. Those who do not recognize this instrumental causality in Mary reduce the dogma of her divine motherhood to nothing more than a *flatus vocis*. Or again, Mary is the co-redemptrix, and this would not be true if she had not effected the Redemption by her own efficacious activity; anyone who denies this is in fact denying her co-redemption.

In short, the speculation concerns words, in utter disregard for their meaning as seen against the sources of the faith and the history of salvation, so that in a one-sided fashion every possible conclusion is drawn from them. The danger of this method lies in its losing contact not only with the content of revelation as such, but also with what the First Vatican Council lays down as the essential preoccupation of theological reflection, namely, the double standard of reference to the total meaning of dogma, and to the meaning of human life as determined by its supernatural end (Denzinger, 1796). We shall not, therefore, be astonished to find that such speculation on words taken completely out of the context which determines their true meaning gives rise to distorted excesses.

As a continuation to this analysis a few words will suffice to put into its place the notion of "development of doctrine" which has been given such a place of honour among Marian theologians. There is a good deal of justification for this: Marian theology, together with sacramental theology, is the part of dogmatic study where development is most manifest. But we must not allow ourselves to be carried away by this into giving mariology the special mission of stimulating future development. The particular section which has most developed up to now is not necessarily that which will develop most in the future, and it is questionable whether the past should be transplanted in this way into the future. The balance of theological wisdom and the *homogeneity* which is the essential characteristic of this "development" throw some doubt on such an opinion.

In any case, such fragile convictions are no foundation for

doctrinal studies. We can be certain of a basis in truth, on the contrary, if we devote ourselves to showing the essential homogeneity of dogma across the diversity of its expression in different periods. This is a fruitful undertaking which has been insufficiently pursued in mariology.

4. DEVOTION

I shall not linger in my consideration of the subject of devotion. The questions raised by the operative factors in this domain are so delicate that I had to set out the principles for their solution in the course of examining them in the preceding chapter.

All I have to do now is to recapitulate these principles and complete them.

The "central peak" of Marian devotion will be found somewhere between the opposite extremes of mariocentricity and mariophobia. It will be christocentric, according to the constant tradition of the Church. Nevertheless, we shall be on our guard against the obsessed and over-scrupulous approach of those who imagine they can see "mariocentricity" everywhere. An example of this can be seen in the way some people feel obliged to be cool in their attitude to Lourdes because Mary appeared there without Christ. Now, if one thing is quite clear to those who go there on pilgrimage, it is that at Lourdes the Eucharist and more and more the Liturgy are at the centre of everything. There, as in many other similar places of pilgrimage, Mary effectively leads to Christ. It would be just as stupid to think that every phrase about Mary in a sermon or a prayer should be accompanied by a clause which attached her to Christ. This could easily become something of a mannerism or a mania. True christocentricity does not lie in such details; it lies in a deep and fundamental orientation. This is what must be recognized and encouraged without any holding back.

The high peak of true devotion is, once again, situated in between superstitious practices and complete abstention from any practice at all, between an excessive or warped emotionalism and coldness or bitterness. Its characteristic is a simple affection, completely subordinated to faith as the essential, and a well-ordered body of devotional practices.

All this comes down to the following first rule: Marian piety must be theological, and, therefore, founded on an authentic theology. This is what preserves it from indigence as well as from deviations and superstitions. In other words, devotion is not situated on the level of sentimentality, but of faith, hope and charity.

Marian devotion can be simple provided it is strong, free provided it is well orientated. To this end, here, as in the realm of theology, it is the essential and not the accidental which must be brought out, dogma and not opinion. Objective piety must be given precedence over subjective, authentic tradition over ingenious innovations.

On this last point, one of the difficulties is that allowance must always be made in matters of piety for the corrosive action of the rule *Quotidiana vilescunt*, which is another way of saying: familiarity breeds contempt. Habit and custom make the essential seem colourless. Something has to be contrived to combat this fatal process. But this does not make every innovation legitimate; any that are gratuitous, superficial or subjective are to be looked on askance. What is contrived must not take the place of what is essential, but give it its true value; it must not draw affection away from primary concern, but lead back to it. This is how to gauge the value of the prescriptions and the "pious undertakings" proposed by the spiritual authors of the last few centuries. The golden rule in this matter is that the renewal must as far as possible not be an innovation but a restoration of forgotten values. Christian tradition is very rich, and the disuse into which so much has fallen presents wide possibilities of restoring things to the light. As an example, Marian piety, which had decreased so much among the younger generations of the post-war years, has undergone an unbelievable renewal through the restoration of pilgrimages, particularly to Chartres, a pilgrimage of which Péguy was one of the initiators. The decreasing observance of Mary's month which has been so evident in the last few decades need not leave us short of ideas. One positive factor which is worthy of attention is often one of the chief causes of it, the very rich liturgical season of the Ascension and Pentecost. These feasts suggest that we should give primacy of place to the Holy Ghost at this time, and so it is possible for private individual devotions to be eclipsed by this celebration. There is nothing to prevent Advent from being made the Marian season of the year, if only in those years when May is a bad month because of occurring Festivals. This would not only avoid devotion to Mary going against the main stream of the liturgy, but it would also mean finding in the liturgy itself a biblical and theological support of great richness for it. This is particularly true of the Marian Masses of the Advent Ember Days, in which we see one of the most ancient and profound appearances of Mary in the official worship of the Church. Marian piety can in this way find a sure foundation outside the cycle of the saints, in the temporal cycle which is the very backbone of the liturgy. By this particular expedient the foundation in Scripture furnished by the ancient Advent Masses would be recovered, and at the same time Marian devotion would return to its first source, the mystery of Christmas, and in that to true christocentricity. I am not speaking purely theoretically in all this, for on several occasions, without wishing to set myself up as a model, I have had pastoral experience of using this solution in a chaplaincy which I once held.

If Marian devotion will only conform to the example of Mary and to her true desires, it will of its own accord lead to Christ, it will be a way to him; it will be real contemplation and not daydreaming, it will be exacting and not facile, it will be action and not quietism, a source of Christian initiative and not a refuge for the infantile. All these are tests by which the authenticity of any Marian devotion can be measured.

The Blessed Virgin Mary is fundamentally she by whom here below, in our humanity so direly in need of salvation, the Incarnation of Love was brought about, in the sense in which John writes: "God is Love" (1 John 4. 16). Prayer and devotion to Mary must therefore lead to an incarnation of love, enabling it to take shape in real life, in the fullness of human and ecclesial reality, in the spirit of Mary's *Fiat* and following her modest suggestion: "Do all that he tells you" (John 2. 5).

V

The Ecumenical Problem[1]

PERHAPS the most outstanding advance made during the pontificate of John XXIII was the revival of a concern for unity. For centuries we had seemed to see only the negative aspects of this problem and particularly the dangers inherent in it, but now it has been set by him on the path of a constructive dialogue.

This does not cause the dangers to disappear automatically, however, and one such danger consists in stating the Marian problem purely and simply in the terms of the separated brethren, as is often done today. To look at the problem solely from this angle would only serve to make it more obscure.

Once the mind is dominated by the idea that Catholic doctrine on the Virgin Mary constitutes a stumbling-block for the ecumenical dialogue, the temptation inevitably arises to water down this doctrine with the sole aim of facilitating union. Now, the desire to be "generous" towards separated Christians should no more become a criterion of theology than that of being "generous" to the Virgin Mary. Theology must rise above both varieties of sentimentality. Unity, of course, cannot come about through compromise, but only through a joint search for the whole truth. Ecumenism must, therefore, be subject to the criteria, and not set up as a criterion itself. If it is ever allowed, consciously or unconsciously, to fulfil such a role. the only outcome will be a return to a constant jockeying for positions, in which truth will be betrayed. What we so direly need is light.

Faced with this threat, many mariologists react in the same context but taking the opposite line. They optimistically suggest that the development of the Marian movement, far from harming the cause of ecumenism, can do nothing but serve it. Their argument is that Mary desires unity, and that she is powerful to forward it. The Church's teaching authority cannot disagree with itself and it does, after all, encourage the promotion of both the ecumenical and the Marian movements. The fullest truth is necessarily for the good of the Church. Marian and ecumenical commitment, therefore, do not run counter to each other, but ultimately converge. The facts which seem to be against this conclusion can only be superficial; the ways of God, which are secret and impenetrable, do not always coincide with our human plans and negotiations.

The fundamental principles of this kind of argument are justified, but the application of them is factitious and mistaken. Basically this attitude has one thing in common with the preceding one: it allows itself to be fascinated by the apparent good of a limited cause, forgetting in consequence to take in a wider perspective and make its own, objectively, the whole range of criteria and facts. This complete view would impose the abandonment of slogans and comfortable routines.

Utterly distinct levels of reality are found lumped together in this attitude: the Marian doctrine essential to Catholicism in the fullest authenticity of this doctrine, and mariology as it is seen on the shelves of the modern library; true Marian devotion and Marian devotion as it appears in practice, with its defects and its excesses; Marian piety in itself, which is *essentially* good, and the appearance it presents to the Protestant or Orthodox observer, due allowance being made for their point of view.

If the mariologist abstracts from these distinctions, thinking that the *Marian movement* has only to keep going along the line which it is following at the present time without any revision, and ecumenism will be forwarded into the bargain, he is under an illusion.

There are the lessons of history. The Blessed Virgin does not always prevent her devotees from falling into excesses and error, nor these defects of theirs from hindering the cause of unity as well as the Marian cause itself. There are apposite remedies which might be applied, as we have seen in the foregoing chapters. The failure to recognize these facts can lead to serious aberrations. Thus it is not unknown for well-intentioned people to hold Marian processions in Protestant villages or towns, with banners and hymns, piously hoping that when the Virgin Mary is thus introduced into their midst she will miraculously bring about their conversion. In actual fact, such manifestations, the planning and conduct of which give grounds for criticism by liturgists and wits, constitute a provocation and only serve to stir up hostility towards the Virgin Mary and Catholicism. These were not the methods of a St Francis de Sales, nor of a John XXIII.

If we must beware of superficial views tending to push Mary into the background for the sake of the ecumenical cause, we must also beware of those which would fail to come to terms with the considerable point of difference which the Marian question constitutes not only between us and the Protestants, but also, whatever may be said to the contrary, between us and the Orthodox.

The catch-phrases which are current on this topic are of two opposing kinds, and, curious as it may seem, they can often be found on the lips of the same speaker, in the course of the same conversation.

The first is that we shall never achieve anything with the Protestants. They are heretics. "You cannot even be sure that they believe in Jesus Christ." Any attempts made in their direction can only result in compromise, or corruption of the Catholics, with no result from the other side. The only way, therefore, which is open to ecumenism is to state clearly the nature and the defects of the heterodox positions, and to expound the Catholic doctrine that non-Catholics would have to accept if God invited them to become converts.

The second catch-phrase is just the opposite : "All is well." We have the same faith as the Orthodox, we are united to Mary, and all that we do to develop doctrine about her and veneration of her can only reinforce the links between us. In regard to the Protestants also, the advancement of the Marian movement as it exists today is the best means of resolving the problem. The signs of a rediscovery of the Virgin Mary among Protestants are the fruit of the development of the movement in its most committed form. For instance, the definition of the Assumption made the Protestants think, and put the problem of Mary squarely before them. It made them develop in the right way. In this vein someone even wrote that Protestants, seeing a man so intelligent and outstanding as Pius XII define this dogma, cannot have failed to say to themselves : "If such a man believes it, it must be true." Nothing could be further from what actually happens both psychologically and sociologically. On the Orthodox side, as we shall see, Marian developments and promotions in Catholicism have been resented as deviations and often as errors. Among Protestants they have been seen as the advance of a fundamental heresy and as heart-breaking proof that there is nothing to be done with the Catholic Church. This at least is the dominant reaction.

It is important to show the illusory foundations on which prejudices like these are built.

In the first place, there is the one-sided concentration of attention on catholicizing authors. This is nothing but pointing out that one swallow—which does *not* make the summer! A Protestant out of line with the majority makes a certain declaration or writes an advanced book in a catholicizing vein. He is cited as being typical and representative of Protestantism, even though he is disowned by his own community. Thus a certain "Dresden Manifesto" in which "Protestants" declared themselves in favour of Lourdes and Fatima because of the miracles happening there, was widely reported in the Catholic press of the world in successive translations, in Italy, France and elsewhere. Letters and a visit to Germany, attendance at meetings of the German Marian Society, which is very much awake to ecumenical affairs—none of these led me to the origin of this "event" which passed completely unnoticed in its own country. What is abundantly clear is that it represents nothing, or at least nothing of any importance.

Secondly there are the exaggerations. If a Protestant of good will, engaged on ecumenical work, should concede this or that point, this concession is taken out of its context, exaggerated, and given a meaning and an importance which it just does not possess. A Protestant or an Orthodox might write that he does *not deny* the truth of the Assumption, and all too easily it will be said that he is *favourable* to it. If he goes so far as to say that he *tends to that opinion*, then he is said to adhere to the *dogma*. If he says he is satisfied with a particular explanation of Catholic doctrine, he is said to agree, or even to be enthusiastic about it. What we might call "take-over bids" such as these harm the cause of ecumenism just as much as a frankly aggressive attitude.

What these catch-phrases have in common is that they illustrate the tendency to let oneself off any real examination of conscience and any real dialogue. Now, it is certainly dialogue that John XXIII encouraged. This dialogue is not a matter of argument and polemic, nor does it deal in illusion and compromise. It is before everything else an attitude of charity in truth (for the first necessarily involves the second). It implies, therefore, a loyal, lucid and positive understanding, knowing particularly the proper way to understand without prejudice the historical situations which condition the conflicts of the present day and the dynamic of unity which has made itself manifest in recent times. A true dialogue implies knowing how to look for, and discover, the means which favour a coming-together towards the full truth.

Certainly reunion can be no more than a long-term hope. It is not yet even on the horizon. And the Marian problem, together with the Papacy and for analogous reasons, is the cause of the most deeply-rooted disagreement, at least for Protestants. But unity is the formal desire of Christ, and, for this reason, it must be the object of our hopes and efforts. In order to throw some light on the possible ways of approach in what concerns the Marian problem, I propose below a few guiding rules. The last of these leads on to an objective examination of the basis of the Protestant and Orthodox positions.

The first rule : Examination of conscience

No dialogue can be undertaken unless there is an openness and a humility on the part of every Christian and every particular group in regard to its own particular lights. It presupposes an examination of conscience in the course of which the faith has been stripped of its impurities in order that what is essential in it may be revigorated. To this effect a perspective is needed which will allow the distinction to be made between dogma and mere opinion, between the Catholic faith and purely personal preferences or the views of a particular school, between authentic devotion to Mary and abusive forms of it. It is important to get outside the mentality of a particular period or country in order to see more clearly the "substance of dogma" beneath the "outer covering",[2] as John XXIII said, and to get in their right perspective the more or less necessary methods of conceptualization, reasoning and presentation which are in honour in our Latin West. Briefly, Catholicism must not be allowed to be confused with recent and transitory fashions in, or actually erroneous forms of, Marian theology or piety. The Church may be infallible, but individual Catholics are not. Each must humbly refer to the sources of his faith of which he always falls far short in some way, either by default, or by the intrusion of alien elements. This leads us on to a second rule, this time a positive one.

Second rule: The law of return to the sources

At a far deeper level than the dialogue, what matters is a return to the sources, because this is a prerequisite of its fruitfulness.

There has never been any success in the ecumenical dialogue along the path of compromise and surrender, nor along that of belligerent argument; success comes only through a return to the common tradition. If the "dialogue" is not fed from both sides by work along these lines, it will soon use up all its resources.

Here again we must beware of catch-phrases. What matters is not the *phrase* "return to the sources" which has been so bandied about and abused that it will end by passing as a synonym of fluidity, but the exacting reality that it covers.

A long-term effort is needed with no hope of success except after many years of objective work. It consists in a return to the one source, Christ the Revealer, by a long and patient investigation of the "sources" of our faith, and in the first place Scripture, using all the means of science and fully alive and open to the inspiration of the Holy Spirit.

In this approach we must first strip from certain doctrinal formulations everything about them which is peculiar, out-dated or in any way tainted; this is the negative aspect of the process. Those who have attempted it know very well that it is not a backward step nor a sweeping-away of all the valid doctrinal progress of the centuries. They know, on the contrary, just how much can be revealed in the process: unexpected rays of light on the unalterable truth and real transfigurations of it.

On the Catholic side, this return to the sources helps to clear away certain particular conceptualizations or formulations which might lead to abuse by being set up as the common doctrine from which standards can be drawn, simply because they have appeared in one or two manuals. A wider, deeper and more complete concept of revealed truth results (although, of course, our understanding of this will always remain inadequate). Formulae which are perfectly justified but have become narrowed are restored, and reinterpreted in the context of a richer whole. The return to the sources will be of particular importance in dealing with many loose or metaphorical uses of the words mediation and co-redemption, and more widely, with the Marian teaching of the most recent popes. To situate this in its place in the line of the Scriptures, the Fathers and the tradition of the Church since then, in order to appreciate its value and full meaning better, will be a most important task. Even dogmatic formulae can be the object of such a study. Needless to say, they are not reformable, but since they can never be *adequate* to express the Mystery, there is room to reset them against the background of a wider whole, more comprehensive in both the logical and psychological meanings of that word. Thus, a return to the sources of the doctrine of the Immaculate Conception could help to get beyond the obstacles so keenly felt in it which today arouse, as we shall see, the concerted opposition of the Orthodox. In short, work of this kind would ultimately *re-centre* all Marian doctrine in the true tradition of the Bible, the liturgy and the Fathers. What has been done in this direction has already borne fruit.[3]

On the Protestant side, it is a fact that such work tends to help on not only a relaxation in certain combative attitudes but also to produce a real rediscovery. Thus an unbiased attention to the true content of Scripture has contributed towards overcoming certain negative and hostile attitudes towards the Virgin Mary, just as the study of St Paul has brought about some escape from the rigidity of certain views on the doctrine of "faith alone" and even of some of those on "Scripture alone".

But we must not allow ourselves to be deceived:

1. There is still a tremendous way to go, especially so far as the Virgin Mary is concerned. But great possibilities now lie open even here.

2. The return to the sources, undertaken in a spirit of loyalty and openness to the entire truth and docility to the guiding of the Holy Spirit, enlarges the basis of what is common to separated Christians, but it is not for this reason necessary for the work to be done in common. Indeed, what is most important in the results of study along these lines is, perhaps, achieved for each in the framework of his own communion. The result is indeed thrilling when the work done on each side converges, like the meeting of the two teams that excavated the tunnel under Mont Blanc. Nevertheless, no one would deny that dialogue is useful, and that it can inspire the investigation of certain avenues of research and facilitate the joint possession of work that has

already been done or is now in the course of completion. In all this, work takes precedence and "words for the sake of words" are fruitless; yet these are what those who wish to launch out into the dialogue without deep and laborious preparation are reduced to.

The discussions at the Council of Florence (1439) and the way they progressed are very instructive in this respect. The dialogue there did dissipate certain prejudices, strengthen common convictions and lead to the signature of an act of union, but this was only because certain of the Fathers had thoroughly studied the sources in advance. The discussions between Scholastics and Byzantine theologians, on the contrary, had the opposite effect of hardening their differences. Moreover, the absence of any deep roots among the ordinary faithful, plus the play of social forces, hopelessly compromised, as we know, the very real fruits of this dialogue.

Third rule : A clear and comprehensive knowledge of each other

The necessary basis for taking part in any dialogue is a knowledge of one's partner's positions and their origins. It is outside the scope of this book to give a detailed exposition of the diverse and sometimes changing positions of each individual theologian on each point of doctrine; that would take us an eternity! What we must do is to grasp the root of the differences which have to be resolved.

Every human opinion, even when it is mistaken, has as its deep driving force the search after some truth. The study of all doctrines, whether human or religious, must be guided by the identification of this truth. It is from this starting-point that the factors of error can be grasped and defined : error like all evil being a negative thing, a privation, and not a positive reality. The ecumenical action *par excellence* consists in two things : grasping with a clear and lucid sympathy the need to refer in this way to the truth (and this reference is the driving force of every system and the secret of its power), and situating everything else in relation to this reference.

The object of the following pages will, therefore, be to set out the authentic aims which should be in view, the significance of the deviations which have compromised them, the disagreements which have resulted from them and the ways by which they may perhaps be overcome. This will not lead us to fail to recognize how grave the differences of opinion are, and how long the journey that still remains before the ultimate aim is achieved.

We shall consider, in broad outline only, first, Protestantism and, then, Orthodoxy.

Relations with Protestantism

On relations with the Protestants, the illuminating fact of history is the sad state of theology at the time of the Reformation, the many abuses, fossilizations and superstitious practices which cried out for reform at the beginning of the sixteenth century. Adrian VI recognized the fact without beating about the bush in his letter of 15 September 1522, to the nuncio, Chieregati, who had been charged with finding a way out of the German crisis: "You shall tell them that we readily (*ingenue*) recognize that God has permitted this persecution of his Church because of men's sins and above all those of priests and prelates. . . . Therefore . . . you shall promise that we will apply ourselves whole-heartedly to the reform, first of all, of the Roman Curia, from which, perhaps, the evil has spread."[4]

The Reformation sprang from a need to re-centre Christian life on certain fundamental and essential values which badly needed restoring. But its promoters, handicapped as they were by the nominalistic theology of the times, and carried off by their re-forming zeal, came, as a result, to the divorce that we know so well. The rigidity of their reactions often threw out the under-lying truth as well as the abuse. Exclusive opinions arose which the Catholic Church could not and can never accept.

This happened in Marian matters. Differing in this from Calvin, Luther professed a very positive devotion towards Mary. He not only held fast to the doctrines of the motherhood and virginal integrity of Mary, but also to the as yet undefined doctrine of the Immaculate Conception.[5] As we have already seen, it was his reaction to very real and tenacious abuses which was one of the reasons for his progressive and never indeed complete aliena-tion from this love for the Virgin Mary.

To this must be added—and it is fundamental—the interplay of those principles which are all characterized by the use of the word "alone": Scripture alone, grace alone, faith alone, God alone. All these principles arise from a similar desire, to return to the essential, to clean up and to purify, which was the positive mainspring of the movement. Had it kept hold of this positive approach and relinquished its peculiar exclusive emphases, Protestantism could have remained a Catholic movement, like the great reform movements of the twelfth and thirteenth centuries.

Let us examine these main principles one by one.

Scriptura sola. The return to inspired Scripture which is the very word of God was surely one of the necessary means of authentic reform. The return came about as a reaction and an exclusion made all the more rigid by the crisis which the life of Tradition was then undergoing. The Marian piety of the time had been invaded by a whole host of corrupt traditions which very largely masked and compromised the true witness of Tradition. Tales of miracles, private revelations and legends circulated in large numbers, laughable and superstitious prescriptions for salvation were put forward. All this cried out for something to be done. A return to Scripture *alone* might have proved an educative means for the particular need of the moment, just as in the Catholic Church today purely biblical gatherings are held— a kind of cure by Holy Scripture; but the particular exclusive emphasis was maintained and held up as a standard. Now, the living link between Scripture and Tradition cannot be neglected (particularly in Marian theology). Not only is Scripture the object of Tradition in the sense that the Canon of Scripture is transmitted (*traditur*) to us by the Church, but also in the sense that Tradition passes on to us its meaning and interpretation. Until the recent invention of printing, preaching, like the teaching of theology, too, for that matter, had been fundamentally the presentation and explanation of the Scriptures. It was in a large measure from pondering on the contents of Scripture, at least as a starting-point, that Tradition had successively made explicit the dogmas of the motherhood of Mary, of her virginity, of her perfect sanctity, and that, at that time, the notions of her original sanctity and her final assumption were in the course of definitive emergence.

Exclusive recourse to Scripture in such a climate was conducive to the rejection of these two doctrines, as yet undefined, with the whole jumble of contemporary Marian excrescences.

One after another, her continued virginity after childbirth, of which Scripture alone does not furnish undeniable proof, her holiness and the expression "Mother of God" which is not in Scripture in so many words even though equivalent statements are, were all called in question.

Faced with so grave a problem the first thing to do is to throw over the adage on which both Catholics and Protestants agreed without difficulty in the sixteenth century—the silence of Scripture on the subject of Mary. Both sides used it to their own advantage : the Catholic side as an excuse for the free development of a mariology with no reference to Scripture, and certainly not to those texts which certain mariologists have rather strangely called "anti-mariological" (Mark 3. 31-5; 6. 1-6; Luke 11. 28; John 2. 4), but which nevertheless are a real and positive part of what the Scriptures have to say about Mary. The Protestants used it as an excuse for neglecting and in extreme cases showing positive disrespect towards the Mother of the Lord. These sad facts of history determine the programme for ecumenical work in the matter—it must include a reaction against this false adage and its evil effects, a return to the Scriptures and an objective search for all they tell us about the Mother of the Saviour. "To rediscover the Virgin Mary *in* the Bible, while the Protestants are discovering her *through* the Bible" has always been for me one of the guiding principles of my work and very often on this particular issue it has borne more fruit than I could ever have hoped.[6] It is a fact that the rediscovery of the Virgin Mary which has gone on among Protestants in recent years has been facilitated by the need felt among Catholics to study the Bible, not with a view to using it as a basis for syllogisms and the construction of systematic arguments, but to discover its true content. It is an acknowledged fact that in this research they have found a very fruitful source of ideas suggested by Protestant authors who are deeply imbued with the spirit of Scripture (I have in mind particularly the fine commentary on the *Magnificat* by Luther, and articles published in the last few years by Protestants like Hebert and Hoskyns). This exchange is all the more fruitful in that it brings to the fore the positive points of agreement not only on the texts but also on methods and principles of interpretation.

In spite of this, no Catholic would think of making use of the

Bible only. It is clear that the fullness of Marian doctrine involves a reading of the Scriptures in the context of the Tradition which is their living setting. This fullness cannot be shared by those who reject Tradition to trust in "The Book" in itself. For what is a book in itself? Has anyone ever taken this approach to its logical extreme? Can a book be read from no particular point of view? The sight of the first Reformers hesitating between varying approaches of each of which it is claimed that they lead to an authentic apprehension of the meaning of the word of God makes this doubtful. Luther sees in the Scriptures the true savour of Christ, Zwingli emphasizes that they are apprehended by the enlightenment of the Holy Spirit who opens their true meaning to men, while for Calvin the main point is the objective inspiration of the very words of the text, a position which shows him to be the nearest of all to the Catholic doctrine.[7]

Reflection on this problem has led large numbers of Protestants to rediscover Tradition, but they still refuse it any normative value. It is important to co-operate with this line of thought in order to present in as favourable a light as possible the openings by which the Protestants might be able to come to accept the demands which Tradition makes. It will become easier for them to do this if Tradition is presented to them not as an independent source completely separate from Scripture but, in accordance with the teaching of St Thomas and of all ancient tradition,[8] as that very act by which the Holy Spirit delivers in and through the Church not just the actual words of Scripture but also an understanding and interpretation of them which go far beyond the words.

The Reformation's second exclusive approach was *gratia sola*, grace alone; in other words, God's gift is of a wholly gratuitous nature. The starting-point of this idea is of profoundly vital necessity for the faith of the Church. At the beginning of salvation in general and at the beginning of the salvation of each individual there is a purely gratuitous grace, without anterior merit. Then, there is no supernatural work which is not *entirely* the work of grace.[9] The Reformers were right in wanting to restore these truths against the Pelagianism and semi-Pelagianism which are always reappearing. (How many Christians are still tainted with these heresies without knowing it!) But here again the Protestant reaction was too radical. The exclusive *sola*, justified in respect of the first grace, is excessive when used in connection with the development of the life of the Christian and of the Church

In the first place man co-operates with the grace which he welcomes and freely makes his own, so that salvation, which is entirely and without exception the work of grace, is also, at the same time and in a subordinate fashion, entirely the work of human free will.

In the second place, this flowering of grace in the life of the Christian produces merit. Of this it must also be said that it is entirely the work of God and entirely the work of man, gratuitous under the first heading, worthy of new gifts in return under the second, for the freedom of God's gift is the very opposite of anything like paternalism. It *gives* us the power of *meriting* glory.

Following this train of thought, the Virgin Mother of God is the most perfect realization achieved by the absolutely gratuitous favour of God's lovingkindness (cf. Luke 1. 28) and the matchless masterpiece produced by his mercy. Thus he gave it to her to reach the highest degree of co-operation, the highest merit which could be had in the Church of the redeemed. Catholic theology could not think of giving up either her co-operation or her merit.

Nor must it fall into that excess of anti-Protestant polemic which tends to give to this co-operation too absolute a value and to harden the idea of merit, so that the fundamental gratuity of grace which is its source is at times completely neglected. "In crowning merits, God is crowning his own gifts," says a proper Preface of the Saints used in France. Certain nineteenth-century liturgists wanted to delete this phrase which to them seemed suspect. It is in actual fact a quotation from St Augustine in which what is most essential in Catholic doctrine is expressed. This essential element must be made as clear as possible.

As we have already seen, any temptation to make grace a material concept must be resisted, any temptation to make of it a kind of substance that is deposited in the soul, after having been previously laid in stock in a heavenly treasury from which the Virgin Mary and the saints draw it to give it to us. Such imagery as this must obviously be got into the right perspective. It has already been explained in what sense it is important to restore the fundamental notion of uncreated grace, that occupation of our souls by God of which created grace is in some way the trace. This is not to deny that there exists in the soul a sort of spiritual organism, or rather an organic elevation of the faculties, which makes the soul capable of accomplishing in a stable and permanent manner divine acts of faith, hope and charity. Thus refocused, Catholic doctrine concerning the grace of Mary and her co-operation in the work of grace can no longer provide grounds for reproaches of anthropomorphism and of injuring the sovereignty of God.

So then, the means of getting beyond the difficulties in these matters will be, on the Catholic side, a return to essentials and a renunciation of any too rigid and one-sided presentation of the doctrine; on the Protestant side, they will take the form of a discovery of our human co-operation in the work of salvation in the humble status of total dependence which is that of man. Christian experience of what God can raise up in man, from within those who live by the life which he gives them, has already made easier certain rapprochements in this field.

The third exclusive approach is related to the preceding one. The Christian is justified by faith alone, to the exclusion of works.

There is here again a valuable emphasis expressed in so many words in St Paul: "It is by faith that we are justified." But the exclusiveness added "alone"; and this, together with the tendency to reduce faith to an assurance of one's own personal salvation, when it really implies an adhesion to the saving truth in its entirety which blossoms in charity, must be rejected.

The paradox of this exclusive approach, so narrowly linked with the preceding one, is that it leaves the economy of the New Testament on the same level as that of the Old. Under the Old Law man was justified by faith in signs and figures of what was to come, not by the sacraments, that is to say by signs conferring grace, infallibly communicating it to those receiving them in faith.

The real trouble here is a depreciation of the *first eschatology* in favour of the second. These two eschatologies, undifferentiated in the Old Testament, but distinguishable in the New, correspond to the two comings of Christ: the first, which has already occurred, in the humility of his earthly life; the second for which we wait, in the glory of his Parousia. The first is already a realization of the last times; it inaugurates a new condition in which grace is communicated to us by the power of the risen Christ. The second is the passage from this economy of grace to the economy of glory. The eschatological promises of the Old Testament are, therefore, accomplished to an important extent in the New Testament, not only by the full revelation of the truth, but by the sacraments wherein the power of Christ the Saviour is really exercised. This is no longer an economy of pure signs, as was the Old Testament, but of real communications.

This latent misconception of the constitution of the New Dispensation goes far towards explaining the misunderstanding of the Virgin Mary among Protestants and how this can go side by side with the positive aspects of Marian thought which they sometimes accept and develop.

The Protestants have no difficulty in admitting the spiritual gifts given to Mary, as to Peter and the apostles, but this they see as being in the same manner and on the same level as for the saints of the Old Testament. At times they will praise the faith of Mary and her humility as a "handmaid", following Luke 1-2. But they consider these gifts to be limited in time, and limited too to the person who received them, not going beyond her. For this same reason, even if they recognize the gifts and privileges given by Christ to his apostles and to Peter, they hold they are limited to the persons of the twelve, and not transmissible. Catholic doctrine differs from Protestant in this above all, that it holds these gifts to be durable, permanent, transmissible, and capable of an effective radiation of their power in the economy of salvation.

It would be true to say that, according to the Protestant point of view, Mary, like Peter and the apostles (and the humanity of Christ, in a certain sense), is an eloquent sign of the grace of God, but they do not participate ontologically in it any more than they are the agents by which it is bestowed. "Abraham, Mary, Peter are types of witness and not types of communication, figures of weakness, not of plenitude," writes Pastor G. N. Rousseau.[10]

It is a fact that the exclusion signified by *fides sola* has largely been left behind among Protestants today and this can be attributed to a return to biblical sources which includes a deeper study of St Paul. And here again the experience of Christian life shows those Protestants who have consecrated their lives to Christ, that faith, adhesion to his word, bears fruit in effective charity and in good works which are such that they cannot be ignored. There is even in this order a remarkable efficiency in Protestantism which in its fashion has been a factor in getting beyond *fides sola*.

Our hope must be along these lines, and we must find an approach in which the scheme of things is Mary's, the scheme of fructifying and co-operating grace which is the scheme of the New Testament, may find its right place.

All these exclusive criteria which are in process of becoming less rigid—Scripture alone, grace alone, faith alone—are fundamentally only the different modes of one, more radical than them all—God alone.

Here again the Reformers were right in their drive to reinstate the transcendence of God in a position of honour. This is a fundamental requirement which is all too easily forgotten and set aside. Catholic theologians and mystics are constantly trying to recover it. "I am he who is, you are that which is not" is a Catholic formula.

The point of conflict lies in the radical extreme to which the exclusive approach is taken, the extent to which it refuses to man the value which God deigned to grant to him. Here we reach the root of all the preceding factors: Scripture *alone*, i.e. refusal to accept Tradition which grows from the work of man; grace alone, i.e. refusal to accept merit in man; faith alone, i.e. refusal to give any worth to man's works. At the bottom of all these lies a single identical refusal to give any value as such to a creature. This position shows clearly in a formula which, although usual among Protestants, is by its form somewhat disconcerting to Catholics: "In the matter of salvation, God is always the subject never the object; man is always the object never the subject."

Simplifying the thought a little we may say that the words "subject, object" indicate respectively "active" and "passive"— a subject exercising an efficacious activity, on the one hand, a pure capacity to receive, on the other. From this springs that devaluation of human actions which we have already noticed. Going a little more deeply, it might be interpreted: "God is always the end and never the means. Man is always the means and never the end." Catholicism can go quite a long way in this direction. It is true that God is the end *par excellence,* indeed that he is the only end in itself, to which all others are completely subordinate and relative. The point at which the parting occurs is that, on the Catholic side, man can only be a relative and a subordinate end; on the Protestant side, he can be no kind of end at all. Now, the single fact that we are the object of God's love is in direct opposition to this rigorous view, for all love in some way considers that which is loved as a subject and an end. Such is the *agape* of the Lord, the *agape* he demands that we should have for each other (Matt. 25. 44-5). This is where the *relative* cultus which Catholics accord to the saints, and among them to Mary in first place, fits in.

Any devaluation of what is human included in an affirmation of transcendence along these lines implies automatically a devaluation of Christ's humanity. Certain circles among Protestants have not failed to face this fact frankly: "If—and this is not to be doubted—Protestantism is at the moment undergoing a crisis," wrote Jean-Louis Lebas,[11] "is it not because its affirmation of the Incarnation has itself become un-incarnated?"

If the concept *Deus solus* is rigidly pursued it leads to Nestorianism. It devalues at one and the same time the humanity of Christ and the divine motherhood of Mary, together with the grace and the efficacy they convey. Thus Mary counts for little among Protestants.

In 1945 Karl Barth set out the key to this antithesis, saying that the whole of Catholicism springs from the analogy of being.[12] If Mary gives her consent in the name of the whole of human nature. and plays this notable role in salvation, it is, he diagnosed, because Catholic theology sees a true resemblance between reasoning creatures and God. Barth held this recognition of the analogy was a misunderstanding of transcendence. The way the problem is posed by him is both profound and enlightening. It pushes to its farthest limit what certain Catholic mystics have felt and formulated just as strongly, but less radically, when they call God "the wholly other": wholly other than man, without anything in common with him. It might be a good thing to encourage in Catholicism the spiritual intuition implied in this formula; the tendency to bring the notion of God down to an almost insultingly anthropomorphic level is a very serious thing.

This intuition of God's transcendence ought not, however, to exclude analogy altogether. It is "complementary", as Karl Barth today recognizes. In saying "ought not", I am not putting forward a philosophical standard extrinsic to Revelation, for this analogy comes to us from Scripture itself. God created man "in his own image and likeness" (Gen. 1. 26-7; 5. 1; 9. 6). It is because of this that man has a true relationship with the Word who is "the image of the unseen God" (Col. 1. 15; 2 Cor. 4. 4; Heb. 1. 3). Thus, precisely as Christ works salvation not in and by his divinity *only*, but in and through the co-operation of his humanity, in the same way he allows men to co-operate in their own salvation, and the highest and most profound co-operation is that of the first of the redeemed, the Virgin who gave birth to the divine Saviour.

In this matter Catholic theology can allow all that is profound and life-giving in the Protestants' intuition, that is, in a word, the transcendence of God. This can form an antidote to the tendencies of the Counter-Reformation, namely the slipping away from the incarnate into the carnal (from Fra Angelico to Rubens), from intellectualism into rationalism, and so on.

The "analogy" of faith must not, however, be abandoned, but it will be expanded by the study of the biblical and patristic sources. This is the way in which the Blessed Virgin's characteristic quality as a privileged figure of God will be fully restored to her.

Continuing this work in the biblical field will not in any way oblige Catholic theology to dispense with a sound philosophy. How can anyone reason without philosophical concepts, whether they are avowed or not, whether they agree or not with the spirit of the Bible? Without going into any technicalities, the full solution of the debate demands that the philosophical difficulties implicit in all the problems should be overcome. In any opinion, the original nominalism of Protestantism had a great effect upon all the attitudes adopted four centuries ago. A sound philosophy (conscious of the division between essence and existence) imposes the following perceptions, which to me seem important: transcendence, far from denying any value to man, to his liberty, his responsibility or his merit, *causes him to exist*, liberates him, gives him the capacity of co-operating with grace and, by so doing, bestows merit on him. The difference between God's transcendent action towards men, and that of one created person on another, is that God acts on his creatures on the level of the first cause, and that means on the most intimate level that can be. His creating and saving activity has the effect of bringing them to themselves in their own proper existence with all their modes of existence, including freedom. The freedom is not an alien thing because God gives it. On the contrary, it is God who causes it to exist as such, makes it aware of itself and creates it in its proper being as liberty.

In what concerns this last and most fundamental principle—*Deus solus*—it is again Scripture, together here with a certain experience of life with God, which will straighten out the inextricability of a series of exclusions sprung originally from a defective philosophy, and will impose the liberating intuitions which we have mentioned.

Orthodoxy

If we now take a look at the question of Marian theology amongst the Orthodox, we shall be tempted to say, in contrast, that the differences here are negligible "We are of one mind about the Virgin Mary; she unites us," is generally the way the situation is stated from the Catholic side. The Orthodox are not at all sure of this. Rather the opposite; they feel utterly out of sympathy with Catholic mariology, and their opposition to it takes just as lively a form as that of the Protestants.

This situation has come about only recently, and only taken a permanent, decided shape since the definition of the Immaculate Conception in 1854. This is a paradoxical state of affairs, for from one point of view the agreement in Marian doctrine between Catholics and Orthodox is deep, and, apart from a few shreds of misunderstanding, might well seem complete.

This must be gone into further. The grounds of the Protestant opposition are completely alien to the Orthodox point of view. At least in what concerns *gratia sola*, *fides sola* and *Deus solus*, the Orthodox position goes beyond the Catholic. Indeed, the temptation to fall into exactly the opposite error to that of the Reformation would seem to be not altogether absent. Protestants insist on the absolutely gratuitous nature of grace to the exclusion of all value in human works. On the other hand, one of the temptations which menace the whole Eastern tradition is a definite inclination towards Pelagianism—an exaltation of Mary's merit to the extent of obscuring the gratuitous aspect of her grace. Nicholas Cabasilas goes far along this road, Demetrius Chrysoloras perhaps even further when he writes: She "had acquired . . . a spiritual beauty greater" than that of "the first man . . . *not by grace but by her own effort*".[13] Certainly most Orthodox would feel this was a little exaggerated, but it does, nevertheless, illustrate a strong temptation for the Eastern mind.

We saw that Protestantism erred on the side of Nestorianism. The great temptation of the East has always been Monophysitism. Protestantism tends to reduce our economy of grace to the scheme of the Old Testament; the Easterns feel that in a certain way they have already entered into the state of glory. The Catholic position, in this case, would seem to be in between the two—nicely balanced. This antithesis between them is however a little masked in the special field of Marian theology because here Orthodox theology has to an extent neglected its own sources and welcomed the influences of Protestant thought. This has come about because of the separation from Rome and the common opposition to the infallibility and the primacy of the Roman pontiff.[14]

However that may be, the Easterns have, in their own tradition, a very lively perception of the triumph of grace even in this life, notably in the Blessed Virgin. Whilst the Protestants scarcely accept anything except the theme of her humility as a handmaid, the Orthodox raise her up as Queen and cover her with endless praises, in some of which even Catholics would now and then feel a certain difficulty in following them.

The ecumenical problem is, therefore, completely different as between Catholics and Orthodox, and Catholics and Protestants.

The last paradox is that it is, in fact, much rarer to find Catholics who have an exact understanding of the Orthodox (who are in principle so close) than it is to meet Catholics who are familiar with Protestant positions. We seem quite satisfied with nothing more than an ignorant and distant admiration, catch-phrases and illusions, notably the illusion that there is no problem in dealing with the Orthodox. Those who have some experience in these things have to suffer from continually hearing a great number of foolish statements on the subject.

Let us try to see a little more clearly how we may best take up the ecumenical dialogue.

If we take our stand strictly on dogmatic affirmations reduced to their essentials, the generally accredited idea of an almost complete agreement can, after a fashion, be justified. But, even on this level, the qualifications necessary are more than mere nuances.

While there is no difference in what concerns those dogmas already accepted at the time of Chalcedon—the divine maternity and the virginity of Mary (although the Orthodox are sometimes put off by some of our Latin formulations and precepts) the same is not true of the two dogmas recently defined.

On the Assumption, the basic agreement is indisputable. The feast bearing this name comes to us from the East together with the first theological reflections on the corporeal glorification of the Blessed Virgin, already current in the sixth century but not accepted in the West until much later, for all practical purposes in the twelfth century.[15] In spite of this the dogmatic definition did not fail to arouse reactions among the Orientals. Certain of them have raised the question whether it is a dogma. The explicit answers tend to conclude that it is rather an opinion (a *theologoumenon*) and criticize certain details of the formula as defined by Pius XII. The use in this matter of papal infallibility has naturally intensified the negative character of these reactions; but as concerns belief in the corporeal assumption, there is no real problem.

The same is not true of the doctrine of the Immaculate Conception. Here again it is to the Orient that we owe the feast consecrated to this belief. Appearing in the seventh century, it did not pass to the West until the twelfth. But it must be recognized that the Easterners' theological reflection on this mystery is vague in the extreme. They are generous with their epithets, but the difficulties of the problem are neither raised nor solved, very much the opposite. They willingly qualify the *conception* of Mary as *holy* or *immaculate*; but one is left wondering when one sees these same epithets applied to the conception of John the Baptist when it is his feast.[16] The thought is, at least, completely positive and laudatory; it gives glory and is, sometimes, quite significant.

We have to wait until the fourteenth century (the time of the

I

triumph of Scotism in the West) to find an Eastern author, Nicephorus Callistus, speaking explicitly of an original stain in the *Theotokos*.[17] This is the starting-point for a retrograde development. The denial of the Immaculate Conception becomes predominant among the Greeks from the middle of the seventeenth century, and among the Russians during the first half of the eighteenth. This process of development had reached its term in the nineteenth century. The definition of 1854 only served to harden the position out of opposition to the dogmatic authority which Pius IX had exercised in the matter.[18]

Surely one would not be wrong in thinking that there is a misunderstanding somewhere here? The whole logic of the Marian doctrine and piety of the Orthodox seems incompatible with the affirmation that there could ever have been a stain of sin in the all-immaculate (*Πανάμωμος*), that she could ever have been a vessel of wrath and the object of divine displeasure. Doubtless, the manner in which the doctrine has been formulated and proposed by the Latins, mentioning both the precise moment when the divine operation took place and its mechanism, the instant of the union of the soul to the body—no less—even alluding to the *infectio carnis*, and finally the style of analytical argument used—doubtless all these factors have provided the motives for this disaffection. When the question arose, the Eastern tradition no longer had sufficient energy to express the same mystery in its own way. This is a pity, for the Eastern genius could have helped the West to find its way out of more than one impasse, and helped it to separate the mystery from the useless details from which it has been found so difficult to isolate it.[19]

There is here a grave problem whose key must be sought in the Eastern conceptualization of original sin and the relationship between nature and supernature. With the Orthodox, nature is a whole, and their way of expressing the role of grace is very different from ours, completely upsetting all our Latin ideas.

The problem of this difference of approach, mentality and outlook between the East and the West appears again over a third issue which has not yet been defined, but of which many mariologists want to promote the definition. This is the whole question of Mary's part in redemption: her co-redemption, her mediation, her spiritual motherhood as we say in the West. The term "co-redemptrix" has a thoroughly foreign ring in Orthodox ears. Any analogous expressions they may have are found to be used in a very different context and spirit. In any case, the title seems to them to be one of the strangest of Latin inventions. The title of mediatrix, which comes to us from the East, is, on the contrary, accepted, but the Orthodox are disconcerted by the way in which we use it and the importance our mariology tends to give it—the importance of a central role, the appearance of a complete thesis. This, in their opinion, puts the mystery out of focus and robs it of its true nature. Finally, our insistence on Mary's motherhood of all men, and, above all, of the Church, puts them off just as much. Though affirmations of this spiritual motherhood are not altogether absent among them, it must be recognized that they are extremely rare, sporadic, and indeed exceptional.[20] The title of Mother of God strikes them with such a force that it suffices in itself, and if, by some chance, they come to the idea of a spiritual motherhood, it is in some way in the orbit of this central mystery and is given no particular emphasis. The doctrinal development which is so intensive among Catholics on all these points and the language of the papal encyclicals which deal with them, are, therefore, an undeniable cause of difficulty for them. Here, at least, there has as yet been no defining of dogmas. The dialogue can be carried on in complete openness, without that feeling of facing an unscalable wall of separation, which is so strong among the Orthodox when brought up against those matters where the Roman Church has made a doctrinal definition.

The important thing is to get in the right perspective the points from which the differences between our Latin mariology and the Marian doctrine of the East spring. Here we shall find the explanation of the divergences, the oppositions and the misunderstandings which we have just had to point out.

From the point of view of sources and method in theology, the Scriptures and the liturgy are fundamental among the Orthodox. Everything is to be found there; there is scarcely anything that does not come from these two, or even, that goes beyond them. From this arises the opposition felt towards that type of Marian theology in which the liturgy had little place, the Scriptures were used in a peculiarly Latin way, and the weight of recent Latin traditions was very heavy and all pervasive. The current effort to return to the sources in Catholic Marian theology is such as to reduce this difference of approach. Still, the fact remains that Eastern thought as well as Eastern Marian piety is completely steeped in a liturgy which is extremely generous in its expression towards the Theotokos, and thus preserves in their full vigour all the most ancient and most traditional ideas, whereas, as we know, a certain kind of Latin piety is seen to be only too prone to the multiplication of subjective devotions, together with the promotion of abstract titles and sharply defined privileges.

Finally, the intellectual climate, the attitude of mind and the perspective of thought differ very deeply

Oriental thought loves mystery, Western, analytical clarity. Marian thought in the East is contemplative and poetic. Its inventiveness consists in translating the same basic facts into continually renewed symbols which give new brightness to the truth and, now and then, bring out—or suggest—some hidden aspect. Latin Marian thought (above all, the most committed) proceeds, on the contrary, by analysis, comparison, reasoning, syllogism. It distinguishes, constructs, forms notions and words answering to the divisions of its rational analysis; it is by choice specialized, systematic, and organized into theses. Finally, it has a way of multiplying juridical notions with which the Orthodox mentality often finds it impossible to cope.

As regards the object, oriental thought keeps to the point of view of the mystery: the Revelation made in Christ needs no more than this centre. Mary is never separated from the Incarnation. She is seen inside the mystery, as forming a part of it. She is the sign of it, the privileged witness to it; she shows it forth. Thus she is the key to the most sacred figures, even to the burning bush and its flame. Following this line of thought there is no hesitation in applying to her texts from Scripture which in the most formal manner signify the divinity of Christ.

"Hail, throne of flame, . . . in you *the fullness of the divinity did dwell corporeally*," says the Acathistos Hymn,[21] applying to Mary Col. 2. 9.

"*We have seen her glory, the glory as of the only* Mother of God, *full of grace and truth*," says Isidoros Glabas, transferring to Mary the words of John 1. 14.[22]

These daring flights of fancy spring from the fact that Mary is seen as the sign that contains and makes manifest the Incarnate

Word, the ikon in which it is venerated. The Orthodox feel no need to say that Mary is "totally relative to God", for this very relation is the whole of their Marian theology. It is part and parcel of their thought and they are little inclined to analyse its terms and foundation, the *esse ad* and the *esse in*, as we Latins love to do. For them it is quite simply the inexpressible heart of the mystery about which they refuse to practise what seems to them something like vivisection.

This is why our logic-chopping with its theses and questions so annoys the Orthodox. This is especially true of the way in which we detach, as a distinct order of questions, Mary's mediation and co-redemption, without any mention of the mystery of the Incarnation (examined elsewhere). In a similar way they find fault with our iconography for representing our Lady without Christ.

Psychologically, methodologically, conceptually, the division between us is deep.

Here, once again, the work of the ecumenical dialogue will be a return to the sources, to the Scriptures and the Greek Fathers and Byzantine homilists, who are also our Fathers. This is a rather wide foundation, but it would be important for both sides to take part in this work, and to a certain degree jointly, for in the last few centuries Orthodox theology has also neglected its own tradition. Such a work would, therefore, lead to the recovery of important things by both sides. On the Catholic side, it would enrich our sense of what the Mystery is, and of the manifestation of God in humanity of which Mary is the sign. It would lead us to look again at not a few recent and particular notions which we tend to handle without reserve, as if they were absolute and adequate. (Thus, the distinction between objective and subjective redemption on which is based the whole question of "co-redemption" in modern mariology is itself an importation from Protestant theology.) In general, the Orthodox would reject any work on the subject which gave the impression of setting up structures and quasi-autonomous functions having in themselves their own efficacy quite independently of the God who works all things in all men. In a dialogue established along these lines, it would have to be shown in what sense our Latin formulae are modes of expression basically equivalent to what the East expresses according to another pattern of thought. It is only at the expense of much work and a long dialogue that, in Marian theology as in other matters, we shall together come to the fullness of Catholicism.

On the Orthodox no less than on the Protestant side, the task is, then, difficult and immense. The end is not yet in sight. Here and now ecumenism must be very careful not to give way to a facile naïveté, and even more careful to make itself docile to the guidance of the Holy Spirit, who alone is able to give an efficacious inspiration to the work, the patience, and the charity needed on each side, and bring them to their proper conclusion.

Epilogue

To give back to the Church its youth, its purity, its vitality, to wipe away the "stains" and the "wrinkles" which men see on its face today, such is the programme which John XXIII gave to the Ecumenical Council. Only then, he explained, shall we be able to present her to all separated Christians saying: "See, brothers, this is the Church of Christ. We have endeavoured to be faithful to her, to ask of the Lord grace that she may always remain as he willed. Come, come; the way towards our meeting lies open before us."[1]

The Marian question is first and foremost a domestic problem for Catholics. I offer no apology for insisting yet again on this fact at a time when many seem inclined to reduce our Marian difficulties to a straight opposition between two parties. Of these, one is said to be bent on diminishing our Lady's importance in the hope of facilitating a union with the Protestants; the other is represented as valiantly defending the full riches of the Church's teaching on Mary. If things were really as simple as that, the solution would be easy, for there can be no doubt whatever that dogma is the thing of real importance. In no circumstances can it be called in question.

The facts, however, are rather different. To state the problem in this way is merely to turn a blind eye to reality, which is that among Catholic thinkers themselves there are differences and indeed contradictions on the subject of the Blessed Virgin, and these offer the Protestant observer a variety of very different images.

In the past I have sometimes wondered whether I was not, perhaps, exaggerating these differences, but what happened during the Second Session of the present Council was more than enough to quieten any doubts I may have had. The differences were shown to be only too real. During this session, as already during the first, the moment the Marian question appeared on the horizon of the Council's preoccupations, the atmosphere became explosive. Certain persons deployed great zeal in denouncing as a plot against our Lady any effort to present the problems in their true light. Passionate accusations and sentimental appeals on these lines were frequently heard. The net result was a general feeling of uneasiness and embarrassment.

Should the chapter on the Blessed Virgin be dealt with in the *schema* on the Church, or not? This simple and perfectly straightforward question voted on on 29 October 1963 developed into a veritable melodrama. A number of Fathers allowed themselves to be persuaded that if they gave Mary a place in the Mystical Body, they would be diminishing her dignity.

Whence could this impression arise? Its origin lies in a pattern of thought that equates the glory of Mary purely and simply with the magnification of her privileges. These do, of course, make her unique and different from anyone else; and the realization of this fact gives rise to the feeling that the more different she is made to appear, the more she is set apart from all other humans, the more glorious she will be. It has even been said that she was separately predestined and that she was the object of a grace and redemption belonging to a different spiritual species. That being so, it is felt that the best way to manifest her superiority over the Church is to set her outside the Church. Placing her in the Church, on the other hand, is equivalent to bringing her down to the general level, a move that could not fail to deprive her of her privileges, in other words, of what is essential to her.

A similar—though less violent—opposition appeared during the debate on the collegiality of the episcopate. In the same circles Peter was thought of as superior to and outside the College of the Twelve. Their formula was: "Peter and the apostles", as though he were not one of the Twelve. They were loth to say: "Peter and the *other* apostles", because this seemed to put him on the same footing as the Eleven. Similarly for the pope and the bishops. It was disturbing, and perhaps even wrong, to say: "The pope and the *other* bishops." One would probably be right in thinking that it was in order to remind people of this truth, obvious in itself in a way certain illusory glorifications are not, that the pope insisted on the fundamental character of his episcopal ministry. "Bishop of Rome and, *therefore*, Vicar of Christ, Successor of Peter, and, therefore, Vicar of Christ, Pastor of the Universal Church, Patriarch of the West and Primate of Italy," he said on taking possession of his cathedral church, the Lateran Basilica, on Sunday 10 November 1963.[2] If the pope is pope because he is the Bishop of Rome, there can be no question of disrespect if we recognize the fact and again give him this title, even if, strangely enough, it had fallen into disuse until John XXIII.

In much the same way, the placing of the Blessed Virgin outside the Church in order to give her the greater honour is a merely illusory glorification. She is above the other members of the Mystical Body, but in grace and in glory she is in the Body. She is the first member in holiness, just as Peter is the first member in the ministry on earth. To tear a member from a body of which it is a part is to mutilate it, not to honour it, however much one may protest that one is merely setting it up higher, on a pedestal. There is only one use for branches cut from the main vine— burning.

This illustration enables us to set our finger on one of the sore spots of this whole conflict. In the heat generated by the clash of opposing conceptions, there can be no doubt whatever that there is a tendency, on one side, to transform Mary into an idol, and, on the other, to turn with horror from this idol. To be sure, this is an extreme situation attained only in theory, for the Church is careful to exercise an effective restraining influence. Nevertheless, there are people who are only too ready to step on to these slippery slopes, and the more they allow themselves to become involved in this artificial conflict, the farther they are likely to go down the dangerous incline.

The vote taken on 29 October 1963 on including the Virgin with the Church cut through the Council, dividing it cleanly into two equal parties. This break in the Council's customary unanimity aroused feelings of sadness, uneasiness, and even dismay. How could it be that the Blessed Virgin, rightly presented by the *schema* as the Mother of Unity, in whose womb was achieved the fundamental union of God and man—how could it be that she should become such a sign of disagreement? This was the agonizing question. On one thing at least all were agreed : it was quite impossible to begin the public examination of the *schema De Beata Virgine*. With men's minds in such a state the whole discussion would have been useless and unbearably sad.

After a moment of dazed amazement for all concerned, it

became clear that moves were being made in an attempt to achieve a quick, non-controversial solution. The idea was to draw up a text on which all could agree, send it to the various episcopal conferences for approval, and have it passed without debate before the end of the Second Session. The situation was extremely tense at the time when I drafted the epilogue to the second French edition. However I wrote (on 15 November 1963):

"The question, then, is burning enough on the surface, but deep down it is not as serious as many people imagine. Two things must be clear to everyone: by the whole of her being and by all the efficacy of her action, the Blessed Virgin is an objective sign of unity which nothing ought ever to have marred. It is man's fault—not the Church's—if she has become a sign of disagreement. Historical circumstances are to blame for this, historical circumstances exacerbated by national peculiarities."[3]

Since then the situation has evolved more happily. A compromise text was formulated. Six drafts, progressively amended, resulted in the presentation of a conciliatory text, which continued to be improved in an atmosphere of co-operation, made possible by a great deal of patience and self-sacrifice on the part of many and by avoiding points of contention rather than discussing them. It was promulgated on 21 November 1964.

It is perhaps curious that passions were chiefly aroused by the question of the Blessed Virgin's titles, abstract titles particularly dear to Italian and Spanish piety: Mediatrix and Mother of the Church.

Cardinals Bea, Léger and Alfrink had asked that mediatrix be omitted because of its ambiguity and to avoid a new ecumenical difficulty. The end result was a compromise in which the word figures among many other titles in general use (advocate, intercessor), but in such a context that it neither obtrudes nor gives rise to any ambiguity.

As for "Mother of the Church", the Theological Commission had omitted this title, at this stage as at all preceding ones, for the following reasons formulated at the time of the final amendments (October 1964):

The expression "Mater Ecclesiae" is occasionally found in works by ecclesiastical writers, but only rarely, and it cannot be said to be traditional. Moreover, it is complemented by the addition of titles such as "daughter" and "sister" of the Church.

It is clear that we are dealing with a comparison. From the ecumenical point of view, the title is certainly not to be recommended, although it may be admitted theologically. It has seemed to the Commission sufficient that an equivalent term should be found.

The meaning of this is clear : the Commission did not dispute that the title could legitimately be accepted, but it avoided doing so because it had to frame a dogmatic Constitution, the language of which needed to be clear and unambiguous, and because this particular expression is susceptible of various different interpretations, some good, some bad.

On 21 November 1964, the feast of the Presentation in the Temple, Paul VI took the alternative point of view : during his address closing the third session, he proclaimed the title in its true and valuable sense, carefully avoiding all ambiguous and controversial interpretations. This is shown by the following emphases :

1. The Pope stated in precise terms that in this context the Church meant "the faithful as well as the pastors", that is the Church on earth or Church militant, leaving on one side the problem of Mary's maternity with regard to the Church in heaven. He emphasized that in the sense in which he had proclaimed it the title was not "new"—a discreet rejoinder to the Theological Commission's objection.

2. He avoided, no less clearly, the chief ambiguity which the title might have involved : that which would make Mary external to the Church, as a mother is to her daughter, whereas they cannot really be isolated one from the other, since Mary is a member of the Church. For this reason he insisted in precise terms at the beginning of his proclamation, that Mary is a part of the Church, that she is "the greatest part, the best part, the principal part, the chosen part".

3. He recalled equally that Mary our mother is also our sister.

This proclamation, in no way a definition, overjoyed certain groups of Council Fathers, in general Italian, Spanish, and Polish, who would have thought it shameful and scandalous if Vatican II had not added a "new blossom" to the Virgin's crown, to quote the expression used that evening at St Mary Major by Cardinal Confalonieri in the presence of the Supreme Pontiff.

In contrast a group of mainly German, English, French, Belgian and Dutch Fathers felt rather less favourably disposed towards it for three main reasons: the papal proclamation seemed to run counter to the decision voted by the Council assembly; also in such a solemn setting it took on considerable importance and yet was accompanied by an extreme discretion on the subject of the schema on Ecumenism promulgated the same day; finally it profoundly disturbed the Protestant observers who had come to the ceremony without suspecting that they would thereby be associating themselves with an act as repugnant to their sensibilities as to their theological positions.

That day in different Catholic circles I heard both extremely enthusiastic or triumphant comments on the one side and extremely bitter and disillusioned ones on the other. One of the pitfalls which seemed to have been avoided by the Council's patient compromise was once more fully in evidence. For all those present, whatever their views, the address seemed to be reduced to two words, *Mater Ecclesiae*. From what happened it almost seemed as if this term eclipsed the judicious qualifications (obscured by applause), as well as the invitation to renew devotion to the Blessed Virgin, "model of faith and of response to God's every call . . . in complete dependence upon Christ our unique mediator". This part of the address, which had the least attention paid to it, could be a starting-point for the growth and intensification of a Catholic devotion to the Blessed Virgin, which would neither arouse internal opposition nor give ecumenical offence.

Many more new beginnings, much more patience and work is necessary before the Marian problem finds its full and harmonious solution. Vatican II will have been merely one stage in this journey.

In short, if Marian doctrine and devotion are the subject of a certain crisis, it is a limited and recent crisis, one which can be averted and for which the solution is being found.

Let us therefore turn to a more concise examination of the problem which we have tried to clarify both on the devotional and theological levels.

Devotion

Marian piety, Marian devotion: is it not significant that these expressions seem somehow debased by the very use we make of them? Here I am using them in their real meaning of Christian love finding its outlet in veneration. The real solution is simple for anyone who has found it: it is merely a right incarnation of Marian piety. By this I mean its embodiment in true and appropriate practices according to the rules laid down by the Church, always more concerned for the essential than for the accessory, for the liturgy than for devotions, for major devotions than for minor ones, for dogma than for private revelations, for what is common to all than for peculiarities whether national, regional or personal. In this she differs from many of her children who, in practice, put forms of merely sectional interest in the very forefront of their devotion as though they were, in fact, essential.

Compared with the ideal I am expounding, two opposed deviations exist. Firstly, there is a kind of notional piety without acts or expression of any sort; it simply vanishes into nothingness. Secondly, we find a false or even corrupt piety embodied in materialistic, mistaken forms. These can be superstition, sentimentalism or myth (the myth of woman, the myth of the mother). Superstition is a corruption of a genuine rite; sentimentalism, a corruption of faith, hope and charity; myth, a corruption of the true Christian doctrine of man. (This is a doctrine the intrinsic value and ecumenical importance of which we must be careful not to underestimate.)

Let me emphasize once again—for the point is constantly being missed—that the real summit does not lie somewhere between a lack, on the one hand, and an excess, on the other, for strictly speaking there can never be an excess of love for our Lady. It lies between a lack and a deviation. What I am discussing is not an excess of love; it is a mistaken love which cannot but be painful to her who is thus loved in the wrong way, and to Christ also, in whom and for whose sake she desires to be loved.[4]

Doctrine

Here, too, we must look for our summit. There can be no question of prescribing some pale "neither too much nor too little". What we have to do is to give the essential its full value and significance, and by "essential" I do not mean "minimum". Maximalist errors, no less than the others, diminish Mary's stature. The portrait they give is a caricature leaving out some of her traits of real greatness, e.g., her value as our model and exemplar, which the liturgy brings out when it says: "Lead us on. We run drawn on by the scent of thy perfume, Virgin Mother of God."

The truths of dogma provide a good beginning. They can be expressed very succinctly. Mary is the Mother of God. She is all holy; she was not cleansed from sin like other human beings; she was *preserved* unsullied in view of the merits of Christ the Redeemer. She is the perfect virgin, the flawless model of Christian virginity in both soul and body (for virginity both as a sign and as a reality is closely associated with the body). Finally, the Virgin is now, body and soul, in the glory of the Risen Christ. Such are the basic formulae of faith.

Anyone who meets them in such a brief summary as this will be left with a twofold impression.

Firstly, these defined truths are few in number. Something seems to be missing; they tell us nothing in explicit terms about our present relationship with Mary. This is where we must look for the explanation of the need clearly felt by some Catholics to be always asking for new definitions on this subject. The suggestions they make are varied: intercession, mediation, coredemption, spiritual motherhood, etc.

Secondly, these truths focus attention on the more exceptional and startling aspects of the results achieved by the free action of God's grace. Hence it would seem that the general line of dogma and faith does in fact tend towards the accentuation and multiplication of Mary's privileges.

The combined weight of these impressions would, then, lead us to hope for further definitions. But is this really the solution of the problem as stated? Should not the solution be sought rather in the acquiring of a deeper understanding of these formulae which, like all dogmatic definitions, are of set purpose limited in their scope? Should not our task be to discover their full import by means of a thoroughgoing evaluation of the sources of the faith? Should we not try to find out what is meant by their mutual relationships and the wealth of doctrine they each contain? This is intuitively and fundamentally the position of the Eastern Churches. For them *Theotokos* is enough. Sometimes even, they seem to think that the additions made to this by the Latins have done nothing but diminish Mary's true stature. It would be a mistake to imagine that they reduce her to her *simplest* expression. What they are doing is seeing her at her *highest*; there they pitch their tent. The best representatives of this tradition never seem to lose sight of the fact that Mary's virginity, conception in holiness, and assumption, as well as her present relationship with mankind are precisely the virginity, sanctity, conception and assumption of the Theotokos, or in other words, a particularly privileged illustration of the mystery of the Redemptive Incarnation. However, let us not exaggerate. I am not arguing here for a mistrust of formulae, or for an impoverishment of concepts. There is no need for us to be ashamed of our Latin passion for explicit analyses. Nevertheless, do let us see these formulae, always, in their most essential, most theological, most christological light, the light that shines in the word *Theotokos*.

In this we contemplate the most sublime heights of Mary's glory, and, at the same time, the sign and human reality by means of which God actually entered into our tragic story to make of it a history of salvation. In this mystery of the *Theotokos* we see, finally, the relationship, all of grace and love, which God contracted with the holiest, the most receptive, and the most co-operative of all the redeemed.

We are looking for a summit. It must be one that will rise above the partial and tendentious views that exalt development at the expense of tradition, privileges at the expense of functions, and glorifying speculations at the expense of dogmatic significance. On the other hand, it will need to rise above those narrow views which, in effect, exalt certain apparently negative texts of Scripture and Tradition at the expense of dogmatic development, functions at the expense of the privileges they imply, an all too human significance of our Lady at the expense of her significance in God's work.

Unfortunately these norms cannot be expressed in cut-and-dried formulae and, still more unfortunately, they upset people who have not yet reached a stage of comprehension where they become self-evident.

What is needed here is a thoroughly objective exposition, but this would take a whole book. As a matter of fact, I have already written something very like this book. It could, of course, be improved, but it does give all the essentials of what is required.[5] In any case, the object of this present work is not to provide a well-rounded-off theological treatise, but to provoke thought, in the expectation that this will lead to a better elaboration of the material.

That being so, I propose in conclusion to suggest an approach which, though limited, is objective. This should enable us to get beyond all those sectional and annoying positions that have been the matter dealt with specifically in this book, and give us the light we need in order to see the Virgin Mother of God as she really is. Do let us resist the temptation to mount up to giddy heights in an attempt to probe Mary's privileges for their own sake, losing sight completely of the specifically human state of nature and grace in which they have their root and foundation.

Mary's privileges (in close dependence on those of Christ himself) are part and parcel of the most humble and lowly conditions of the common estate of all mankind. Mary herself magnifies the Lord because he has "regarded the low estate" "of his hand-maiden", her "nothingness" in the dramatic language of French seventeenth-century writers. More accurately still, she means her acceptance in the Lord of that low estate, wholly in the spirit of all the "humble poor of Yahweh" whose line culminates in the Blessed Virgin.

This person "blessed among women" was, first of all, a poor, simple woman directly involved in all the want, hard work, oppression, and uncertainty about the future that are inseparable from life in any under-developed country. This under-development was extreme in Nazareth, where a woman's work was a ceaseless struggle for existence from dawn till night. Mary had not only to wash and mend clothes. She had to weave the cloth and, before that, to spin the yarn. She had not only to bake the bread; she had to begin by grinding the flour and, probably, even by cutting down trees for firewood herself. That, at least, is what the women of Nazareth are still doing now in our day. The Mother of God was no queen of an earthly kingdom. She was the wife and mother of working-men. She was poor, not rich. This was because the God-Man was to live in this state, and it was her calling to give birth to him and thus introduce him to his place in the history of mankind. "It was necessary that Christ should

144

suffer" (Luke 24. 26) and die. Therefore, it was necessary that the Mother of God should be the mother of a man condemned to death with all the shame brought on him by the hostility of the populace and the religious and civil authorities of his country. Before that, it was necessary that she should share with him the state of drudgery and oppression common to the vast majority of those he came to redeem, those "who labour and are heavy-laden" (Matt. 11. 28).

This low estate is not only the root, it is also an intrinsic part, of her glory. It is the law of the Beatitudes (Matt. 5. 3-11; Luke 6. 20-2) and, before that, of the Magnificat (Luke 1. 48). To limit oneself to the triumphalistic glorification of a Lady Most Marvellous is to turn Mary into something she never was, some sort of far-off princess. One would even run the risk of turning her into a goddess utterly foreign to our human estate. This would mean the elimination of a basic aspect of the veneration that is due to her. She is not only a higher being whom we glorify and who helps us with the power Christ has given her to share with him; she is firstly a model that attracts us. If this aspect is set aside, the others cannot possibly obtain their full meaning.

On a deeper level, Mary shared the experience of the dark night of faith common to all the redeemed. This was her kind of beatitude on earth, no other: not the beatitude of knowledge in tranquil possession of its concepts, or of ecstatic vision, but the beatitude of the "glass" and the "darkly", as says St Paul (1 Cor. 13. 12); not the "wisdom of the wise", but the "folly of the cross" (1 Cor. 1. 18-19). Christ does not allow her any complacency at all in her human motherhood. Even a mother's most legitimate pride is taken from her. While still a boy, Jesus reminds his mother that one day he will leave her without warning to serve his Father in heaven (Luke 2. 49). When a woman's voice from the crowd exalts in her a too human beatitude, he retorts: "Blessed rather are those who hear the word of God and keep it" (Luke 11. 27-8). And again: "Who is my mother, and who are my brothers? . . . Whoever does the will of my Father in heaven is my brother, and sister, and mother" (Matt. 12. 48, 50). Mary's "better part" is to "ponder these things in her heart" (Luke 2. 19, 51), as words of the Word of God. Her beatitude is the blessedness proclaimed once and for all by Elizabeth: "Blessed is she who believed, for there will be fulfilment of what was spoken to her from the Lord" (Luke 1. 48).

As we have already seen, any attempt to withdraw the Virgin of Nazareth from the darkness of her life of faith in order to exalt her during her earthly existence to the enjoyment of the beatific vision is a mistake. It throws a wrong light on her destiny, and instead of glorifying her, has the opposite effect of diminishing her. The same must be said of the theory that attributes to her a grace specifically different from the grace given to the other members of the Church. Mary's grace comes from Christ's grace and is specified by the same last end. Its sphere of activity is the self-same organism of theological and cardinal virtues. The marvellous thing about this grace is that it represents the flawless plenitude of what Christ effects in his other members to a lesser degree through all the varying fortunes of a life more or less tainted by sin. To make of this grace something different from ours is not to glorify it; it is equivalent to a disparagement of the specific value of the gift God offers us all. In the same way, it is a mistake to maintain that Mary's redemption is different in kind from ours, for it is undoubtedly the redemption wrought by Christ, in its most perfect accomplishment and including certain modalities of anticipation and perfection proper to this one case alone. There is nothing in all this that transfers her to some other φῦλον, some different genus, either in nature or in grace, and though her predestination is closely bound up with Christ's, it is not a predestination of another sort, something that would remove her from among us. On the contrary, it makes her wholly one of us. Her glory, therefore, is not of a kind different from the glory that awaits us and, as such, incomprehensible for us. It is the very same glory as that to which we aspire each of us in his own degree, and even if that degree will never reach hers, all are, nonetheless, in the scale of the same Communion of Saints. Mary is in all things higher and greater than we in the order of grace, but she is other than we in nothing. She is our queen, but we also shall reign with Christ. She is above us only in order that she may be the nearer to us.

It is worth pointing out further that Mary's beatitude was of the kind that comes, not from glorious actions, but from living unheard of and unknown. It was not the satisfaction felt by the Pharisee absolutely certain that there are no irregularities in the

accounts of his things done, but the unassuming fidelity where
the left hand does not know what the right is doing (cf. Matt. 6.3).
The Blessed Virgin must have known better than anyone what
our Lord meant when he said: "When you have done all that is
commanded you, say, 'We are unworthy servants; we have only
done what was our duty'" (Luke 17. 10). Her lot on earth was not
to lead and command but to serve as a "handmaid". This is the
only title she gives herself in the Gospel, and she uses it twice
(Luke 1. 38, 48). We see here why she, rather than another, was
the one to receive the promise of the Master who, so different
from the masters of earth, himself assumes the slave's apron to
serve those who are making ready to serve him (Luke 12. 37; cf.
Luke 22. 27 and John 13. 1-16).

In this case, just as when one reads the Beatitudes or the
Passion according to St John, it is important to lose sight of
neither aspect of the whole reality. We must see both the glory
and the humility. We must see the glory in the humility and,
even more perhaps, the humility as the root and indeed the
human stuff out of which is made the transfiguration into glory
which is God's gift. It is when Christ is "lifted up from the earth"
on the cross as a sign of derision and contumely according to all
human standards that he draws all men to himself (cf. John 12.
32; also 3. 14; 8. 28). It is precisely at the depth of this *kenosis*,
this self-emptying of his humanity, that he shows forth most
clearly "the glory" the Father gave him "before the world was
made", "the glory as of the only Son from the Father, full of
grace and truth".[6]

This is the approach that will keep us from turning Mary's
privileges either into a fleshy glory *à la* Rubens or into the abstract
achievement of a predestination quite foreign to the circumstances of our life in this world.

Nothing could have been more obscure, more unnoticed by
the chronicles of human splendour and magnificence than Mary's
beginnings and her end: the immaculate conception of this
humble daughter of Israel, and God's miraculous action in taking
her to himself, body and soul, at the end of her earthly destiny.
Just as obscure, too, were the secret message brought her at
Nazareth and the maidenly childbirth in the stable in Bethlehem.
If we have really seen all that, then this perception will colour

our understanding of the true nature of the marvels of grace that God worked in his holy Mother. We shall see her compelling attraction as our model and feel a special confidence in her as our merciful Mother, the first of all the members not only in the Communion of Saints, but also in participation in the intentions, actions and glory of Christ, for this very special reason—among others—that she was the humblest of women.

Then too, with the Fathers, we shall see neither her life as a succession of isolated episodes, nor the dogmas dealing with her as a list of truths we ought to aim at lengthening. We shall see rather the unfolding of a plan of immediate interest to us all. God's plan in the world, the salvation of the world, and, in the very first place, God's Incarnation in the world are communicated to us by faith : the fruitful faith of Abraham, father of the people of God, at the very origin of the promises; the faith of Mary, Mother of God, for the ultimate fulfilment of these promises. In the womb of this faith bearing the fruits of charity and service to others "the Word became flesh and dwelt among us". This grace, moreover, given from above, this grace, in kind the same as ours but full and complete, flowers forth into a glory which, in its turn also, is in kind like to the glory God makes ready for us.

The mystery of her who, in the words of St Leo, "conceived God in her mind before she conceived him in her body", gives full meaning to the twofold presence of Mary in the mystery of salvation : her presence before God and her presence among men, both in the fellowship of one life, in one body. Here indeed two utterances made at Cana find their lasting meaning. The first is addressed to Christ, telling him of men's thirst : "They have no wine"; the second, to men, telling them to hope for God's gift and to give it their co-operation : "Do whatever he tells you."

Notes

CHAPTER I

[1] The case of Tre Fontane is, in many ways, a special one. The Church's decision was unfavourable and any public veneration is forbidden at the grotto. But private prayer is not; and public services are tolerated in a neighbouring chapel. The flow of pilgrims continues.

[2] It should be noted that these apparitions of Mary without Christ do give rise to a fundamentally Eucharistic cultus. (At Lourdes, the Mass is the central act of the day, and in the Procession it is the Blessed Sacrament, not the statue of Mary, which is carried.) Everything leads to Christ, fulfilling the proper function of the Marian cultus.

[3] E. Bergh, "Les Congrégations féminines des XIXe-XXe siècles", in Maria, 3, pp. 465-88. Cf. Enciclopedia Mariana, Genoa, 2nd edn 1958, pp. 607-30. This multiplication is all the more remarkable when it is remembered that the Ecumenical Council of Vienne (1312) had already forbidden the foundation of any new religious families, and that this legislation was continually renewed and reinforced over the succeeding centuries. But no decree has ever been able to arrest an historical movement.

[4] The Legion of Mary is still active, but the figures for the other associations would have to be revised today. The renewal and recent progress of the Marian congregations founded by the Jesuits in 1563-4 should be noticed, together with the falling off of the Confraternities of the Blessed Virgin and the Children of Mary, as well as of a number of confraternities which are now little more than a façade.

[5] Enciclopedia Mariana, Genoa, 2nd edn 1958, pp. 638-40.

[6] These figures are taken from the statistics published by G. Besutti, "Bibliografia Mariana", 1948-9, 1950-1, 1952-7, in Marianum, Rome.

[7] Bibliografia Mariana, 1950-1, Rome, 1952, p. 5*.

[8] The references for the texts of Pius XII and John XXIII are given in my report in the Revue des Sciences philosophiques et théologiques, 46 (1962), pp. 330-1.

[9] Louis Veuillot, Mélanges, Paris, Gaume, 1860, vol. 5, pp. 605-6.

[10] One of the most able specialists in current Marian literature, a man of balanced outlook, G. Besutti, puts it very clearly: "Se è crescente il numero degli scritti mariani, pochi sanno utilizzare il frutto delle ricerche dei teologi. Quanti poi scrivono sui santuari, troppo raramente sanno utilizzare le sane regole della critica storica.

Notes

. . . Andrebbe tenuto presente il monito di S. Bernardo: '*Virgo regia falso non eget honore*'." Cf. "Apparizioni e santuari", in *Marianum*, 24 (1962), pp. 315-16. It is a fact that some of the statements found in this literature are at times quite breath-taking. See, for example, those quoted in *Marianum*, 24 (1962), pp. 158 and 292.

[11] R. Laurentin, *Marie l'Église et le Sacerdoce*, Paris, Lethielleux, 1953, Vol. I. The theme studied in this work is the history of the idea of the "priesthood of Mary".

[12] These are the titles of two books much appreciated in the seventeenth century: the first by P. Barry, S.J., Lyons, 1636; the second by Antoine Alar, O.P., Valenciennes, 1617.

[13] The Hebrew word *shuph* is here translated in a rather vague way; it means at the same time the action of the heel against the serpent's head, and that of the serpent's head against the heel. The real meaning of this word, which is only used twice elsewhere in the Bible (Ps. 139. 11 and Job 9. 17), in both cases in obscure contexts, remains uncertain. Much ink has been spilled over it. See R. Laurentin, "L'Interprétation de Genèse 3, 15 dans la tradition", in *Études mariales*, 12 (1954), pp. 75-156, in which I tried to sort out the history of the interpretation of this verse.

[14] It should be noted that Gen. 49. 17 belongs to the same literary tradition (J) as Gen. 3. 15.

[15] Vol. 5, p. 935.

[16] Pneumatology: the section of theology (much neglected in comparison with mariology) which studies the Holy Spirit.

[17] See on this subject Y. M.-J. Congar, in *Études mariales*, 10 (1952), p. 93 and p. 105, note 26.

[18] J. Bonnefoy, "La Mérite social de Marie", in *Alma Socia Christi*, 2 (1953), p. 22; cf. p. 47; Rome, Academia Mariana.

[19] P. Bonnichon, "Pratique de l'enseignement de la théologie mariale", in *Bulletin de la Société française d'études mariales*, 2 (1936), pp. 60-2.

[20] John 10. 18; cf. 13. 1-3; 14. 30; 17. 19; 18. 4; 19. 30.

[21] See on this subject G. Baraúna, *De Natura Corredemptionis Marianae, in Theologia Hodierna*, Rome, 1960, pp. 73-9.

[22] This is the conclusion reached in the work mentioned in the preceding note.

[23] Pius X, *Ad diem illum*, 2 Feb. 1904, *ASS*, 36 (1903-4), p. 454: "A Christo ascita in humanae salutis opus, *de congruo, ut aiunt* promeret nobis quae Christus de condigno promeruit." The clause "*ut aiunt*" refers to the long series of authors who have approved this doctrine in a precisely defined sense, with the categorical exclusion of merit *de condigno* which was judged to be contrary to the faith by Suarez (see below, notes 25 and 26).

[24] "*Audacter dixi* nihil Christum Dominum meritis suis ex condignitate . . . adeptum (esse), quod non etiam Virgo Deipara *ex congruitate* impetravit, si tamen excipias originalem et priman gratiam qua Virgo donata fuit: hanc enim sibi nulla ratione aut congruentia consequi Virgo potuit." F. Chirino de Salazar, *Pro Immacu-*

lata Deiparae Virginis Conceptione Defensio, cap. 21, no. 7 (1st Edn., Alcala, 1621); Cologne Edn., 1622, p. 135A. Salazar refers to his account in his commentary *In Proverbiis* (published in 1618, Cap. 8, no. 215; Cologne Edn., 1621, col. 624), in which he was the first to defend the extension of Mary's merit *de congruo* to all that Christ has merited *de condigno* (with the exception of Mary's first grace).

[25] "Quamvis B. Virgo nec nos redemerit, *nec aliquid de condigno nobis meruit*, tamen impetrando, merendo de congruo, et al Incarnationem Christi suo modo cooperando, ad nostram salutem cooperata est. *Prior pars est certa de fide, quia esse mediatorem dei et hominum proprie ac perfecte solius est Christi.*" Suarez, *De Mysteriis*, I, q. 38, a. 4, disp. 23; Paris edn., 1866, Vol. 19, p. 331, col. 1; cf. *ibid.*, col. 2: ". . . nec nos redemit nec de condigno nobis meruit", and earlier: disp. 18, s. 4, no. 15, p. 298.

[26] "*Non* utique *condignam* et aequalem sed tamen *congruam* et aliqualem . . . obtulisse." Salazar, *Pro Immaculata Deiparae Virginis Conceptione Defensio*, Cologne, 1622. The same exclusion appears in all those who disseminate this thesis: F. Poiré (in 1630), *La Triple Couronne*, 2e couronne, 5e étoile, s. 2, V, Paris, 1656, p. 347: "Il . . . ne convient qu'à Jésus-Christ, Dieu et homme, de satisfaire en rigueur de justice, et de mériter la grâce et la gloire à l'homme disgracié . . . avec condignité." J. B. Novati, *De Eminentia Deiparae*, c. 6, q. 11; Bologna, 1639, p. 234A 2: "De congruo tamen dico quia solus Christus de condigno nobis meruit . . . et mereri potuit . . . solus fuit Redemptor noster." B. de Los Rios; *Hierarchia Mariana*, Antwerp, 1641, p. 67 (marginal heading giving résumé of the development): "Non quod satis dederit aut satisfecerit de condigno, quod solius est Christi." In the same way A. Pintus Ramirez in 1642; G. Tausch in 1645; Diego de Celada in 1648; F. van Hondegem in 1655. This is not the place in which to publish the vast file that I have assembled on this question.

CHAPTER II

[1] H. Barré, *Prières anciennes de l'Occident à la Mère du Sauveur*, Paris, Lethielleux, 1962, p. 22.

[2] R. Laurentin, "Le Saint-Siège et le développement du dogme de l'Immaculée Conception", in *Virgo Immaculata*, 2 (1956), pp. 37-46.

[3] Several times during the nineteenth century the Holy See reiterated a decree forbidding the introduction of new titles "etiam per ephemerides".

[4] See, for example, *Alma Socia Christi*, 1 (1951), pp. 102-4.

[5] G. Jouassard, "L'Interprétation par saint Cyrille d'Alexandrie de la scène de Marie au pied de la Croix", in *Virgo Immaculata*, 4 (1955), pp. 28-47.

[6] H. Barré, "Saint Bernard, docteur marial", in *Analecta Sacri Ordinis Cisterciensis*, 9 (1953), p. 101; L. Modric, *Doctrina de Conceptione B. Virginis in controversia saec. XII*, Rome, 1955, 62 pages.

[7] This legend of Scotus's solemn disputation was introduced by Francesco de Arimini in the sermon *Necdum* which circulated under the name of St Bernardine of Siena; a critical text is published in *Bibliotheca Franciscana Scholastica Medii Aevi*, 16 (1954), p. 370. Note 4 on pages 369-70 retraces the career of this belated legend which A. Emmen and C. Piana, O.F.M., have reduced to such elements of truth as are in it. The merits of Scotus are in no wise diminished by the dissipation of this false glory, rather the opposite.

[8] H. Ameri, O.F.M., *Doctrina theologorum de Immaculata B. V. Mariae Conceptione tempore Concilii Basileensis*, Rome, Academia Mariana, 1954. See especially, pp. 214-49.

[9] R. Laurentin, in *Virgo Immaculata*, 2 (1956), pp. 65-78.

[10] Luther's *Works*, Weimar Edition, Vol. 11, p. 61, quoted by E. Stakemeier in *De Mariologia et Oecumenismo*, Rome, Academia Mariana, 1962, p. 445.

[11] L. Cognet, "La Dévotion mariale à Port-Royal", in H. du Manoir, *Maria*, Vol. 3, 1954, pp. 119-52. See also P. Hoffer, *La Dévotion à Marie au déclin du XVIIᵉ siècle*, Paris, Cerf, 1958, pp. 59-117 and 189-95, in which the author establishes the fact that Widenfeld was not a Jansenist.

[12] *Ep.* 132; PL 33, 508: "Magis linguae certaminibus quam scientiae luminibus."

[13] See for example, C. Dillenschneider, *La Mariologie de saint Alphonse de Liguori*, Fribourg, Switzerland, 1931.

[14] See on this subject the monograph by Hoffer, mentioned above in note 11.

[15] On this controversy, see R. Laurentin, "Le Titre de corédemptrice", in *Marianum* (1951), p. 21, and the list of texts, pp. 56-9, Nos. 10, 113a, 114, 123, 124, 125.

[16] J. Stricher, *Le Vœu du sang en faveur de l'Immaculée Conception. Histoire et bilan théologique d'une controverse*, 2 Vols., Rome, Academia Mariana, 1959.

CHAPTER III

[1] "The Rosary, an Integrist Devotion?" reads a headline in *L'Homme nouveau* on 19 May 1963 (No. 347, p. 16); this strange question is justified there by the following explanation: "At that time I had been told, and had believed, 'Oh really, not the Rosary! That's an integrist devotion!'" As it stands, this comment is nonsensical. The Rosary cannot be called either "integrist" or "progressive", any more than can the Virgin Mary herself. What is true is that certain forms of Marian devotion tend to be taken over by the political Right or by religious integrism. Lourdes, when it first began, was the object of a siege action of this kind: the examination of the first few thousands of letters shows this. As a result, an important aspect of the message was obscured—that concerning the poor, an aspect which has been coming back into the light for the last ten years or

so. In our days, Marian piety has inspired activities based on theses which are those of a narrow anti-communism which is more political than Christian. Our Lady of Fatima had her place on the barricades of the 13 May 1958, and the choice of this date for the outbreak of the revolution of the Algerian French gained much sympathy for this revolution in circles practising a fervent devotion to Fatima. Many expressed the hope that this revolution was the dawn of the great events awaited in 1960, the date when the famous secret was to be disclosed. It is clear that the Virgin Mary had nothing to do with the politics of this affair or of any others. Perhaps we may be excused the painful necessity of producing chapter and verse for these examples which are sufficient to show clearly the processes which tend in this way to compromise the Virgin Mary. She is quite clearly being spontaneously used as their rallying-point by one side to the exclusion of their opponents. It is of extreme importance that we should all give up creating compromising situations of this sort, so deplorable and so damaging both to the Virgin Mary and to Catholicism.

² *Nunquam satis*—"never enough" in what concerns Mary: an adage of the kind of Marian piety that shows a strong tendency to turn itself into a theological criterion.

³ H. du Manoir, *Maria*, Vol. I, pp. 695-706.

⁴ Pius XII, *Radio Message to the International Mariological Congress in Rome*, AAS, 46 (1954), pp. 677-80. These directives have been taken up several times since, notably by John XXIII in the *Apostolic Letter Motu Proprio* of 8 December 1959, AAS, 52 (1960), pp. 24-6. These warnings have had practically *nessuno effetto*, one of the most well-informed Italian mariologists told me recently. It is vitally important that they should.

⁵ J. F. Bonnefoy, O.F.M., "Marie indemne de toute tache du péché originel", in *Virgo Immaculata*; with much verve and little consideration for hurt feelings he attacks such infelicitous expressions as: "Mary sinned in Adam" (Le Bachelet, *DTC*, 7, 1157); "a certain stain (*aliquid maculi*) was found in Mary's flesh, which could instrumentally cause a stain in her soul itself"; "*Total* preservation from original sin seems contrary to the Catholic faith. . . . The Blessed Virgin must have contracted it in some way" (Del Prado, *Divus Thomas et Bulla . . . Ineffabilis*, Fribourg, 1919, pp. ix, 119, 229).

⁶ "She conceived in her mind before she conceived in her body," St Leo, *Sermo I in Nativitate*, 1; PL 54, 191B. On the meaning of this expression see R. Laurentin, *Queen of Heaven*, pp. 89-90.

⁷ With his great pastoral sense, John XXIII felt this problem very keenly. On the occasion of the "Pellegrinaggio delle Meraviglie" which had as its object the solemn consecration of the Italian nation to the Immaculate Heart of Mary by means of a countrywide journey of a statue of Our Lady of Fatima, he sent a message in which he emphasized the importance "of taking the practice of the virtues and the reality of the Christian life more seriously", but in which he scarcely mentioned the consecration. The text of this message has

been left out of the voluminous book of 440 pages consecrated to an account of this pilgrimage : *Il pellegrinaggio delle meraviglie*. A cura del Comitato Naz. Mariano per la consacrazione dell'Italia al Cuore Immacolato di Maria e per il tempio di Trieste, Rome, Ars grafica, 1960. "We can find no explanation for such an omission," notes G. M. Besutti, "Apparizioni e santuari mariani", in *Marianum*, 24 (1962), p. 279.

⁸ L.-M. Grignion de Montfort, *Treatise on the True Devotion to the Études mariales*, 17 (1960), p. 2.

⁹ L.-M. Grignion de Montfort, *ibid.*, No. 103.

¹⁰ H. Barré, "Saint Bernard, docteur marial", in *Analecta Sacri Ordinis Cisterciensis*, 9 (1953), pp. 106-7 : "The Immaculate Conception, the corporeal Assumption, the spiritual motherhood, all three are points of doctrine which St Bernard never professed, although in his time great attention was paid to them" (p. 107).

¹¹ "The Byzantines are not . . . minimalists. They invent titles to the glory of Mary by the dozen, if not by the hundred. Reading some of their homilies, prayers or thanksgivings one is tempted to conclude that Mary is everything for men, except their mother." A. Wenger, "La maternité spirituelle dans la théologie byzantine" in *Études mariales*, 17 (1960), p. 2.

¹² "Jesus wishes to condemn, Mary to save. From Jesus we can look for justice, from Mary, for clemency," E. Binet, *Le Grand Chef-d'œuvre de Dieu, ou les Perfections de la Sainte Vierge*, Paris, 1634, p. 673. It is no exaggeration to say that for all this this author has a "good reputation"; even so well-informed a theologian as C. Dillenschneider calls him a "serious mariologist", *La Mariologie de saint Alphonse*, Fribourg, 1931, Vol. 1, p. 211.

Chapter IV

¹ Two tendencies towards abstraction can be identified. The first, in a christotypical direction, tends to identify Mary with her divine motherhood. For it she would be that motherhood itself. The second, in an ecclesiotypical direction, would tend to turn Mary into an abstraction somewhere in "salvation-history", the essential mystery of the Church (*Wesensgeheimnis der Kirche*), or even "transcendent femininity" or "the eternal feminine" in the finest meaning of the phrase, as mentioned in the preceding chapter. The dangers of such abstractions were brought out by Ida Friederike Gorres, *Nocturnen, Tagebuch und Aufzeichnungen*, Frankfürt-am-Main, 1949, pp. 132-3.

² There are eighteen quotations from eleven different authors under this heading in H. Marracci, *Polyanthea Mariana*, republished by J. J. Bourassé, in *Summa Aurea*, 9 (1862), col. 1085. The context, of course, is no more open to misunderstanding than that of John 10. 34-5 : "You are gods", a text which is quoted by many of those authors, whose constructions, it must be acknowledged, belong to the realm of pious fantasy rather than to theology.

³ "Finally, the complement, and in a certain way, the fourth per-

son of the Blessed Trinity," O. Van Den Berghe, *Marie et le sacerdoce*, Paris, 3rd Edition 1875, p. 32. A note quotes: "Hesychius, *Serm. 2 de Laudibus V.*, and Mgr Malou, *L'Immaculé Conception*, Vol. 2, p. 175." The latter does, as a matter of fact, praise the use of the title "fourth person of the Trinity . . . because the processions of the divine persons, if this term is understood in a wider meaning, are only completed by the birth of the Incarnate Word on earth". This is why, he adds, certain expressions "to some extent make a divine person of her" (*ibid.*, p. 176).

⁴ That is to say a proximate or remote debt of sin, as we saw above, Chapter 1, p. 21.

⁵ On the use of this expression in the eleventh and twelfth centuries, see H. Barré, *Prières anciennes de l'Occident à la Mère du Sauveur*, Paris, 1962, p. 188, line 96; p. 256, line 5; p. 276, lines 2-5: "Sancta Maria, te laudo, te adoro, magnifico et glorifico. Laudo et adoro altitudinem tuam. Laudo et adoro gloriam tuam. Laudo et adoro speciem et sapientiam tuam, etc." The classical distinction between the worship of *latria* reserved to God, and of *dulia* or *hyperdulia* for the Virgin Mary, is found in Suarez, *De Mysteriis*, I, q. 28, a. 4, d. 22, *De Adoratione B.V.*, Paris Edition 1866, Vol. 19, pp. 323-8. The word is still to be found in N. Nigidio in 1702, and in Sedlmayr (Bourassé Edition, 8, 198-211) in the middle of the eighteenth century. A serious study of this evolution in vocabulary would form a valuable monograph.

⁶ Paul de Vooght, O.S.B., "Le Rapport Écriture–Tradition", in *Istina*, 1961-2, No. 4, pp. 499-510.

⁷ The text quoted is from Benedict XV, *Letter "Inter sodalicia"*, 22 March 1918, *AAS*, 10 (1918), p. 182: "Ita cum Filio patiente et moriente passa et paene commortua, sic *materna in Filium iura* pro hominum salute *abdicavit* placandaeque Dei iustitiae quantum ad se pertinebat Filium *immolavit*, ut merito dici queat: Ipsam cum Christo humanum genus redemisse." In his thesis, under H. Lennerz, *Corredemptrix*, Rome, Universitas Gregoriana, 1939, p. 119, Hermann Seiler comments: "What do paternal or maternal rights over a child really signify? Certainly not a relationship of possession of the child by his parents, in his essence and his existence. It is true that the parents engender the child, and that is why he has a *relationship of origin* towards them. But the child is a *person*, like his parents, and that is why he has absolutely the same rights. . . . The child is not a thing, but a person, and, because of his essence, he cannot be ordered to other men. This is why when paternal or maternal rights are spoken of in common parlance, all that is to be understood by them is a relationship of origin and the duty for the child of filial devotion towards its parents which flows from it, not the relationship of a thing towards its maker. It follows, therefore, that this kind of maternal right is definitely not an effective right. . . . It must, therefore, be said that, in their encyclicals and rescripts, the popes have allowed themselves certain oratorical flights quite without theological foundation (*die der theologischen Grundlage entbehrten*)."

Though Pius XII mentions these rights in a more doctrinal and solemn document, *Mystici Corporis Christi, AAS*, 35 (1943), p. 247 : "Artissime semper cum Filio suo coniuncta, eumdem in Golgotha, una cum *maternorum iurium* maternique amoris sui *holocausto* . . . obtulit", this does not alter the metaphorical character of these rights. In any case, they are presented with more reserve : Mary does not *abdicate* them, she offers them in *sacrifice*.

[8] St Thomas Aquinas, *Summa Theologica*, I[a], q. 1, a. 2.

[9] *Ibid.*, a. 8, and several times later on in the *Summa Theologica*.

[10] The last acceptation here envisaged (principles = articles of faith) corresponds more or less to the thesis according to which the divine maternity is the first principle of Marian theology. Nevertheless, the principle as object envisaged here by St Thomas is the Incarnation. Thus he is discussing formally the principle of christology, and not some special principle peculiar to mariology only implied in the phrase of the Apostles' Creed : "and in Jesus Christ, his only Son, our Lord, who was conceived by the Holy Ghost, born of the Virgin Mary", or in the more developed formula of the so-called Niceno-Constantinopolitan Creed : "Qui propter nos homines et propter nostram salutem descendit de caelis et incarnatus est de Spiritu Sancto, ex Maria Virgine, et homo factus est."

CHAPTER V

[1] BIBLIOGRAPHY ON MARIAN THEOLOGY AND ECUMENISM. An exhaustive bibliography would fill a small volume. The following must suffice for our present purpose :

(i) SOME EARLIER ARTICLES OF PARTICULAR INTEREST :

Y. M.-J. Congar, "Marie, l'Église chez les protestants", in *Études mariales*, 10 (1952), pp. 97-106; J. Hamer, O.P., "L'Attitude des protestants devant la doctrine mariale", in *Journées sacerdotales mariales, 1951*, Dinant, 1952, pp. 125-48; Idem, "Marie et le protestantisme à partir du dialogue œcuméniquen", in H. du Manoir, *Maria*, 5 (1958), pp. 983-1107; A. Wenger, "Foi et piété mariales à Byzance", *ibid.*, pp. 923-82.

(ii) THE PRINCIPAL TITLES AMONG RECENT CATHOLIC PUBLICATIONS :

Estudios marianos, 22 (1961), 496 pp. (reviewed in *Revue des Sciences philosophiques et théologiques*, 46 (1962), pp. 373-5; *De Mariologia et Œcumenismo*, Rome, Academia Mariana, 1962, xii-594 pp.; *Études mariales*, 19 (1962): *Mariologie et œcuménisme: I. Église orthodoxe*, Paris, Lethielleux.

(iii) SOME PROTESTANT WORKS WHICH MAKE A CONTRIBUTION TOWARDS A RAPPROCHEMENT :

H. Asmussen, *Maria, die Mutter Gottes*, Stuttgart, 1950, 62 pp.; W. Tappolet, *Das Marienlob der Reformatoren*, Tübingen, 1962, 365 pp.;

M. Thurian, *Marie, Mère du Seigneur, Figure de l'Église*, Presses de Taizé, 1962, 286 pp. Mention must also be made of a bulletin by M.-J. Le Guillou, "Mariologie et œcuménisme", in *Istina* (1963).

[2] "The *substance* of the ancient doctrine contained in the deposit of faith is one thing, the *formulation* in which it is clothed another." John XXIII, *Address at the Opening of the Council*, 11 October 1962, printed in *L'Osservatore Romano*, 12 October. John XXIII takes up this distinction (which was softened down in the official Latin version made on the basis of the Italian text) in his speech of 4 November, in Italian, published in *L'Osservatore Romano*, 5-6 November 1962 : "It is only natural that the novelty of the times should suggest different *forms* and methods for the outward transmission of the same *doctrine, clothing* it in a new way; but the living *substance* of it is constant . . . the truth of the gospel."

[3] For example the pioneer works of M. Jugie, A.A., are of great merit : *L'Assomption*, Rome, 1944, and *L'Immaculée Conception*, Rome, 1952, completed (and sometimes rectified in various details) by the works (unfortunately now interrupted) of A. Wenger, *L'Assomption de la Très Sainte Vierge dans la tradition byzantine du VIᵉ au Xᵉ siècle*, Paris, 1955, and the works of the same author (cited above) in *Études mariales*, 13 (1955), pp. 43-60, and 17 (1960), pp. 1-8, in *Maria*, 6, pp. 923-982; and in *Virgo Immaculata*, 4, pp. 196-215. This specialist would certainly have been capable of first-rate research-work on the sources. Such work is urgently needed in this field and would be of great profit, not only to Catholics, but also to the Orthodox themselves who, at the moment, show some tendency to ignore their own sources.

[4] Instruction of Adrian VI on the declarations to be made at the Diet of Nuremberg, in *Hadrianus VI, sive Analecta Historica . . . collegit Casp. Bermannus*, Utrecht, 1727, p. 375; L. Pastor, *Geschichte der Päpste*, IV, 2 (1907), p. 93. [English trans., edited by R. Kerr, London, Kegan Paul, 1910, Vol. IX, Chap. 3.]

[5] See on this subject the remarkable study of E. Stakemeier, "De B. V. eiusque cultu iuxta Reformatores", in *De Maria et Oecumenismo*, Rome, 1962, pp. 424-50. The position of the other Reformers, Zwingli (*ibid.*, pp. 450-9), Calvin (*ibid.*, pp. 459-73) is much more negative. On present-day mariology see A. Brandenbourg's contribution, also excellent : "De Mariologia ac de cultu venerationeque Mariae apud Christianos disiunctos protestanticos hoc tempore vigentibus", *ibid.*, pp. 479-516.

[6] This is an allusion to several reviews in Protestant magazines of my *Court Traité de théologie mariale* [English translation : *Queen of Heaven*, Dublin, 1956], as also of *Structure et théologie de Luc*, 1-2; to ecumenical circles in which it has been possible to study these works fruitfully; and finally to the fact that such suggestions and insights have been able to facilitate the rediscovery of the misunderstood content of Scripture in Luke 1-2 by, for example, Max Thurian. I will simply quote this review of *Queen of Heaven* by Richard Paquier in *Revue de théologie et de philosophie de Lausanne*, 1954,

p. 147: "The interest of this work lies for us in its first chapter headed 'Mary in Scripture'. Though the development of Marian doctrine remains unjustifiable from our evangelical point of view, on the other hand, we must loyally admit that the mother of the Saviour holds a greater place in the texts and the thought of Christendom than our confessional viewpoint has allowed us to realize."

[7] See on this subject Stakemeier's study in *De Mariologia et Oecumenismo*, Rome, 1962, p. 474.

[8] See, for example, the study quoted in the preceding chapter, note 6.

[9] This doctrine was affirmed most clearly and energetically by the Councils and the Fathers from the time of the Pelagian crisis onwards. A large number of texts will be found simply by looking up the *Enchiridia* of Denzinger and Rouet de Journel.

[10] G. N. Rousseau, in *Réforme*, 26 May 1951.

[11] In *Verbum Caro*, 8 (1954), p. 1.

[12] K. Barth, *Kirchliche Dogmatik*, 1/2, Zollikon-Zurich, 1945, p. 158. Barth has now revised his former position and no longer rejects the analogy of being.

[13] A. Wenger, "La Nouvelle Éve dans la théologie byzantine", in *Études mariales*, 13 (1955), describes the doctrine of Cabasilas, pp. 50-1, and quotes (p. 56) the text of D. Chrysoloras (*In Dormit.*, Codex Escorial, 164, fol. 76ᵛ).

[14] It is very striking to see the small place given to references to Catholic work and the relatively large place given to references to Protestant writers in recent Orthodox works on Marian theology.

[15] H. Barré, "La Croyance à l'Assomption corporelle en Occident de 750 à 1150 environ", in *Études mariales*, 7 (1949), pp. 62-123. This is the basic article on the subject and is continued in "La Croyance à l'Assomption de 1150 à 1250", *ibid.*, 8 (1950), pp. 1-70.

[16] M. Jugie, *L'Immaculée Conception*, Rome, 1952, p. 139.—N.B. It is obvious that texts referring to the original (passive) conception of Mary in the womb of her mother, the object of the feast of the 8th or 9th December, must not be confused with those concerning the conception of Christ in Mary, the object of the Feast of the Annunciation on 25 March. The texts about the sanctity of the conception in the first sense are ancient and frequent.

[17] A. Wenger, "Foi et piété mariales à Byzance", in H. du Manoir, *Maria*, Vol. 6, p. 952.

[18] *Ibid.*, pp. 954 ff.—Anyone who feels doubt about the harshness of the opposition the Orthodox feel towards the dogma of the Immaculate Conception has only to read the book by A. Merslukine, *Le dogme romain de la Conception de la Vierge Marie et le point de vue orthodoxe*, Paris, 1961. "An erroneous doctrine" the definition of which deepens "the *abyss* which separates the Church of Rome from the Orthodox Church", declares the author on the first page of this work (p. 9).

[19] Thus it was at the last moment, in the work-session he held alone with his secretary Pacifici (1-8 December 1854), that Pius IX

removed the reference to the moment of "the creation of the soul and its infusion into the body" which would have drawn the dogmatic statement into useless and delicate philosophical problems. See R. Laurentin in *Virgo Immaculata*, 2 (1956), pp. 86-7, notes 306 and 311. Inextricable difficulties which had beset the question for centuries were thus eliminated.

[20] A. Wenger, "La Maternité spirituelle de Marie dans la liturgie byzantine", in *Etudes mariales*, 17 (1960), pp. 1-17. See R. Laurentin, in *VIIIᵉ Congrès marial national*, "La Maternité spirituelle", Paris, Lethielleux, pp. 4-8.

[21] Mercenier, *La Prière les Églises de rite byzantin*, II, 1, 2nd edition, p. 351.

[22] *Homily on the Annunciation*, PG 139, 24C.—Doubtless such audacities as these are more to be admired than imitated, but it should be noted that already in Luke 1-2 certain expressions apply to the Virgin Mary an honour which, of itself, belongs to Christ. Of this I wrote: "One might be tempted to find the christocentricity (of Scripture itself) at fault." See *Structure et théologie de Luc 1-2*, Paris, Gabalda, 1957, pp. 149-50. This is an invitation to understand the spirit that lies beyond the letter.

EPILOGUE

[1] "Speech to Italian Catholic Action", in *L'Osservatore Romano*, 10-11 August 1959. The Pope had already spoken on this theme on 14 June 1959, before the students of the Greek College (*Informations catholiques internationales*, 1 July 1959). He took it up again on other occasions.

[2] "Address by Paul VI", *L'Osservatore Romano*, 11-12 November 1963, p. 1, col. 3.

[3] Peculiar national tendencies. This question, which is inevitably raised by international encounters, the reviewing of the publications of various national societies and finally by contacts at the Council, is a delicate one. Newman felt this very keenly. After his conversion he wrote: "Such devotional manifestations in honour of our Lady had been my great *crux* as regards Catholicism; I say frankly, I do not fully enter into them now; I trust I do not love her the less, because I cannot enter into them. They may be fully explained and defended; but sentiment and taste do not run with logic: they are suitable for Italy, but they are not suitable for England." (*Apologia pro Vita Sua*, O.U.P., the World's Classics, p. 202.)

This would call for a special study. Without pretending to any ability to define the *essence* of each national tendency, I propose to point out briefly some of their most obvious and most striking characteristics.

Marian theology in Germany is noteworthy for its attention to roots and sources, to foundations and substructures, to the explicit data found in Scripture and the Fathers. In doctrine its concern with man stands out: the meaning of woman's part in salvation, Mary as the New Eve, her role as representing mankind. It has developed a whole system of symbolism along these lines.

English Marian theology is sober, positive, crystal-clear, opposed to all accretions and, like its German counterpart, concerned with the sources. We can see here certain traits of the English temperament; but we must also reckon with the influence of Newman, in whom the English cast of mind found remarkable expression.

Spanish mariology shows great attachment to its own national tradition. Although it is attempting to enlarge this basis—with considerable success in the case of certain scholars—the national heritage is still what furnishes the essential material for its forward march. This progress is inspired by a concern—sometimes by a very conscious one—for promoting the development of Marian dogma. This school of mariology has provided itself with a solid rational framework and shows a propensity for closely-knit systems of thought. Its temptation is to a certain theological rationalism. Starting from a word or from some title of the Virgin, it proceeds to work out by abstract reasoning all the implications it can be shown to contain, right to the very last. Spanish mariology likes inventing new notions and new expressions. A typical one is Cordimarianism, i.e. the theory and practice of special devotion to the Heart of Mary. If it is true that some (not all) Spanish temperaments love notions like this, there can be no doubt whatever that the two previous peoples find them repellent.

Italian mariology is tender, laudatory and eloquent. It aims at clarity in both concept and expression. In the better cases this results in a crystal-clear limpidity; the less good examples are superficial and fight shy of effort. This is where we must seek the roots of a certain kind of rationalist temptation. Though rationalism is foreign to the deepest resources of the Italian temperament as typified in the admirable enchantment with living we find in a St Francis of Assisi or a John XXIII, it weighs heavily on a whole sector of Italian thought, far beyond the confines of theology. This mariology is frequently long-winded like the Spanish, but it is less systematic. Its verbosity and its fairly general maximalism depend on a criterion proper to Italy, but in Italy often invoked even by official theologians —that of "generosity with the Madonna". (In the last few years this criterion has caused certain works on Marian theology to fail to obtain an *imprimatur* or to be withdrawn from sale.) The Italian school is for ever multiplying the titles of the Blessed Virgin, which it considers like so many "ornaments to her crown" (another typical expression). If even one or two of these are missing, it is felt to be an act of meanness towards the Madonna, something like tearing down a flag from a public building. The mariology of the popes, from Pius IX to Pius XII chiefly, is penetrated through and through with this national tendency even though it does, by all the breadth of its universal catholicity, rise above it.

What are the tendencies in French mariology? Here I must confess my embarrassment. Analyses like these are much easier to make from outside than from inside. The French temperament is, I suppose, characterized by its tendency to pursue one line of thought or action to the bitter end forgetting all about the others. We may follow out our investigations into the positive element so far that we finally lose ourselves in it; or, on the other hand, give our whole interest to speculations showing little concern for the facts. In its best moments, however, French mariology makes a real effort to overcome this, and other similar tensions.

⁴ Mary and the Church's mission. One line of thought seems to me particularly likely to favour true devotion to Mary and, therefore, the union of Christians: Mary is the figure of the Church's mission in the world. Obviously, the Church's mission is not merely to build up from without. Nor is it "psychological action" consisting in stealing or coercing men's souls. It is the beaming forth of a witness of faith, hope and charity. It is presence in the world. Mary who conceived in her mind before she conceived in her body Christ, the eternal Word of God, and who bore him in joyous "haste into the hill country" (symbolical of the resistances and obstacles of this world)—Mary, present with Christ, present where the Spirit is at work (Luke I. 35; Acts I. 14), and finally, present among men, is the perfect figure of the Church's mission and the mission of every Christian. She is the exemplary presence calling forth all that is best in the Communion of Saints.

⁵ R. Laurentin, *Queen of Heaven*, Dublin, 1956.

⁶ John 17. 5; I. 14.—This is inspired by André Laurentin's unpublished thesis, *Jn. 17, 5, La Gloire que tu m'as donnée avant que le monde fût.*